Table of Contents

Table of Contents

Introduction:

Your First Steps Into Canva & Social Media Creation

If you're opening this book, chances are you're standing at the starting line of your creative journey. Maybe you've never designed a post before. Maybe you've tried Canva once, felt overwhelmed, and quietly closed the tab. Or maybe you're already posting on Instagram or TikTok, but your content feels inconsistent, slow to produce, or simply not "you" yet.

This book was written for that exact moment — t**he moment where creativity meets uncertainty, and the desire to grow meets the need for clarity.**

Today, social media is built on visuals. Whether you run a small business, share lifestyle content, teach online, or simply want to appear more polished in your personal brand, people will judge your message by what they see before they ever read or listen. The good news? **You don't need years of design training to stand out. You just need the right foundations** — and Canva has become the most beginner-friendly, accessible design platform in the world.

But being beginner-friendly doesn't mean "basic." Canva gives you tools that creators at every level use to publish every day: layouts, color systems, typography, templates, animations, and more. And in this book, you'll learn how to use them with intention, not guesswork.

This guide is built specifically for beginners and social media creators. You'll learn how to:

- Understand the **foundations of visual design** without the jargon.
- **Build posts, carousels, covers, and simple animations** that feel clean and modern.
- Create visual consistency so your followers **instantly recognize your style.**
- **Use ready-made templates in a smart way** — not as shortcuts, but as creative frameworks.
- **Produce content faster,** with less friction and more confidence.

Each chapter gives you practical exercises, real scenarios, and small wins you can try immediately. Nothing here requires advanced skills or expensive tools — only curiosity, a bit of practice, and the willingness to click and explore.

Whether you're starting a new page, improving a personal brand, or preparing your first pieces of content, this book is your companion for those early steps.

By the time you reach the final page, Canva will feel less like a tool and more like a creative partner — something you can rely on every time you want to express an idea, tell a story, or simply show up online with a little more intention.

Welcome to your new creative beginning. Let's start building.

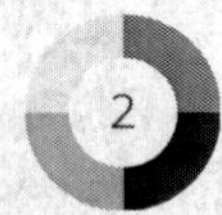

Quick Exercises to Kickstart Your Journey

These warm-up exercises may feel simple, but they plant the seeds for everything that comes next.

By the time you step into Module 1, you'll already have a clear sense of direction, a source of inspiration, and a project in mind that makes learning Canva both personal and purposeful.

1. Map Your Priorities

Take a piece of paper and list the areas where you most need design support: social media, presentations, marketing materials, or video. Circle the top two. This will keep you focused on the modules that matter most to you.

2. Build an Inspiration Folder

Open a folder on your computer (or inside Canva itself if you already know how to do it) and save five designs that you admire — they can be ads, posts, slides, or covers. Don't overanalyze. Just collect what inspires you. These examples will become your visual compass for your next projects.

3. Define Your First Design Goal

In your notebook, complete this sentence:

"The very first thing I want to create in Canva is..."

This is your anchor project — the design you'll keep in mind as you move through each exercise and tutorial.

4. Make Time for Exploration

Block out 30 minutes in your calendar this week to log into Canva and explore the dashboard. No pressure, no tasks — just a walk-through. The goal is to feel at home in the space before we start building.

Module 1 Canva for Beginners

Opening the Door: Why This First Module Matters

Module 1 - Canva for Beginners

Opening the Door: Why This First Module Matters

Most people meet Canva at a moment of urgency: a presentation due tomorrow, a new Instagram post that should have launched yesterday, a flyer your community group needs by the weekend. You open the site, you see a flood of color and possibility, and you hope the software will somehow do the work for you. Sometimes it does—until the next design looks off, the text isn't aligned, or the export is blurry. That's where this module steps in.

Think of Module 1 as your calm introduction to a powerful workshop. We'll slow the pace, learn the layout of the room, and build a few early habits that save hours later. You'll discover that design is not about fancy tricks; it's about clarity: choosing the right format, selecting a readable font pairing, aligning elements so the eye can breathe, exporting in the correct quality so your work looks sharp everywhere. Those basics turn Canva from a "template machine" into your daily creative assistant.

This is not theory. **By the end of the module, you will have produced real work**: a simple logo, a color palette that feels like you, and three coordinated social posts you're proud to publish. You'll know why your decisions work—not just where to click. That confidence is the point. Once you understand the foundations, everything else in this book—social packs, business kits, AI rebrands, short videos—becomes faster, cleaner, and easier to repeat.

Before we dive in, set an intention. What do you most want from Canva right now: consistent social content, a clearer personal brand, or materials you can hand to a client or teacher? Keep that goal in a notebook. You can also use the notes from the previous wxercise. We'll return to it often as we build your skills layer by layer.

In this module, you will:

You're not reading for inspiration—you're reading to ship. Here's the journey we'll take, in plain language, so you can track progress as you go.

- Learn the space you'll work in every day: account, interface, dashboard, and how to find the right template fast.
- Shape your eye with typography and color: simple rules for pairing fonts, picking a palette, and using contrast with intention.
- Structure your page with grids, alignment, grouping, and sensible spacing so everything instantly looks more professional.
- Work with images and elements—uploading, cropping, layering, and using transparency without making a mess.
- Export correctly in PNG/JPG/PDF so your posts are crisp and your print files are clean.

It helps to picture the outcome. This is who you become by finishing Module 1. By the end, you'll be able to:

- Start any project from a template and make it yours—not a clone.
- Manage text, shapes, and images with confidence, keeping layouts balanced.
- Use grids and alignment so designs feel calm and intentional.
- Export in the right format and size without trial-and-error.
- Deliver a Mini Personal Brand: simple logo, palette, and 3 coordinated social posts.

Chapter 1

Getting Started: Your Canva Space & First Creative Steps

Chapter 1

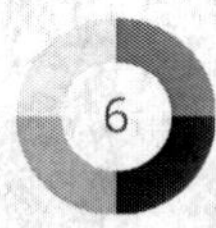

Getting Started: Your Canva Space & First Creative Steps

Every Journey Starts With a Login. Every tool has a threshold moment—the second you open it for the first time. With Canva, that moment isn't about advanced features or polished exports. It's about the very basics: setting up an account that won't get lost, understanding an interface that looks simple but hides layers of power, and realizing that organization is not an afterthought but the foundation of creative speed.
Think of it like walking into a workshop. Before you can build furniture, you need a bench that's stable, tools that are sharp, and a shelf where everything belongs. Canva is the same. The dashboard is your workshop floor. The sidebar is your toolbox. Templates are your starter kits. If you rush past these, you risk building frustration instead of designs.

This chapter slows you down on purpose. We'll focus on four deceptively simple things: creating and securing your account, navigating Canva's interface without guesswork, taming the dashboard with folders before chaos arrives, and learning how to find templates that actually support your vision instead of trapping you in cookie-cutter design.

Why does this matter? Because the speed and polish you'll enjoy later—batching social posts, exporting campaigns, even rebranding an entire business—depend on these early habits. Beginners who skip setup often waste hours later searching for files, fighting the wrong fonts, or losing edits because they worked under the wrong login. Professionals never make those mistakes—because they invest ten careful minutes at the start.

By the end of this chapter, you'll no longer feel like someone "trying Canva for the first time." You'll feel like someone who owns a workspace, knows where the tools are, and understands how to start any project with clarity.

What You'll Do in 10 Minutes (and why it matters)

Before we build anything complex, you'll take a quiet tour through Canva's front door. The goal isn't speed; it's familiarity—because once the interface feels like home, you stop fighting the tool and start thinking like a designer. In this short warm-up you will:

- Create a single, reliable account so every project autosaves and shares cleanly across devices.
- Walk the interface, noticing how tools reveal themselves only when needed.
- Tidy the dashboard with two starter folders, avoiding chaos before it begins.
- Find and open a template that actually matches your intent, so you begin with structure instead of a blank page.

Your Canva Account: The Foundation You Don't Want to Rebuild Later

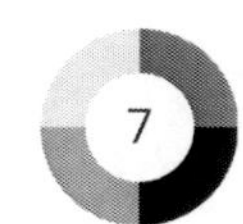

Every creative habit begins with a home.

For your Canva work, that home is a single account you trust. Using multiple emails is like hiding your tools in different rooms—you will eventually lose something important.

Open canva.com and choose Sign up via email, Google, or Apple.

Pick the login you already use for professional or school work and stick to it. When Canva asks why you're here—personal, business, education—answer quickly.

This setting influences the templates you see first; it doesn't lock your account to one use.

Canva

‹ Continue with your work email

Using your work email makes it easier to design together with your team.

Work email

yogaforwomanlife@gmail.com

Continue

‹ Continue to Canva

Continue with Apple

Continue with Google

Continue with Facebook

Continue with Microsoft

Continue with Clever

Continue with email

Continue with work email

Log in with phone number

By continuing, you agree to Canva's Terms of Use. Read our Privacy Policy.

‹ Create your account

You're creating a Canva account with yogaforwomanlife@gmail.com

Name

Continue

Finish signing up

Enter this code within the next 10 minutes to log in to your Canva Account.

809732

You're receiving this email because you have a Canva account. This email is not a marketing or promotional email. That is why this email does not contain an unsubscribe link. You will receive this email even if you have unsubscribed from marketing emails.

Canva

Made for you with ♥ from Canva
Canva Pty Ltd, 110 Kippax St, NSW 2010, Australia
ABN 80 158 929 938 | Privacy Policy

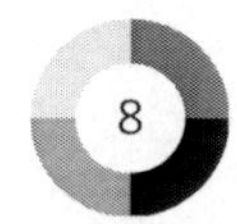

Your Canva Account: The Foundation You Don't Want to Rebuild Later

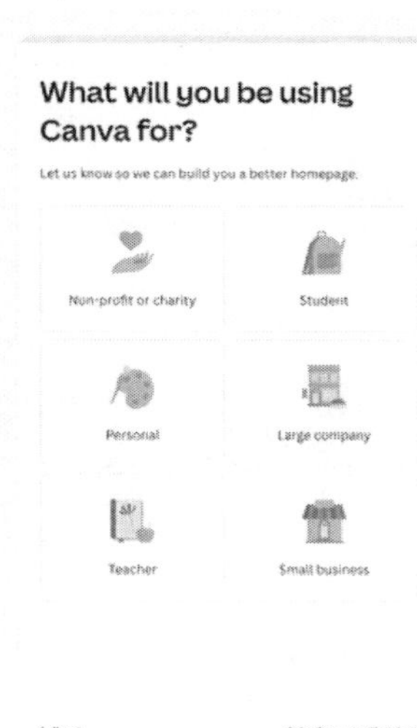

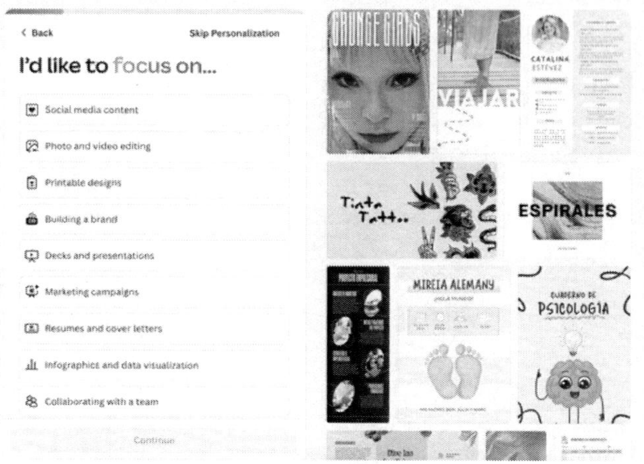

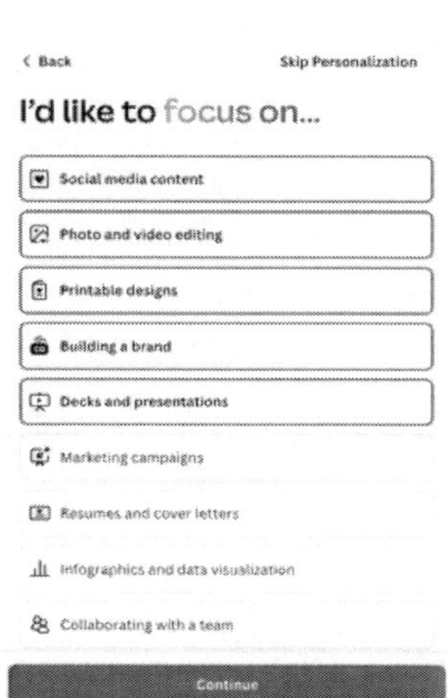

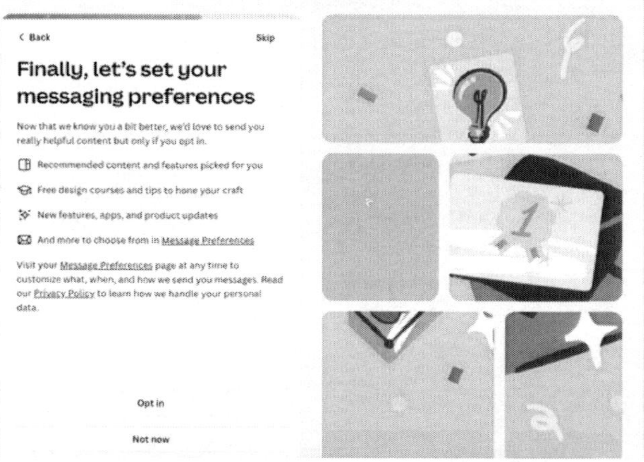

Complete your profile.

Add your name (or brand name) and, if you like, a simple avatar. It sounds cosmetic, but shared files look more credible when the author's name is clear. Later, when you export, that name helps you track drafts and versions without confusion.

Real Scenario — The "Lost Export" Problem

A student designed a presentation over two evenings: half on a laptop, half on a tablet. The slides looked great—until she couldn't find the final version on submission day. Two accounts, two sets of files. The fix was simple: one login, every device. Once she consolidated, the stress vanished. The work didn't change—only the system did.

Pro Tip — Start a Naming Habit Now

Before your library grows, pick a format for file names:

- YYYY-MM Project — Short Title — v01
- ClientName — Asset — Platform — v01
- Type it once; duplicate and update the version number. In a month, you'll thank yourself for the tidy history.

Mini Exercise — Make It Real

Create your account and confirm your email. Then create a blank design and name it: 2025-10 Canva Practice — First Steps — v01. You've just started your test archive.

Understanding the Interface: A Workspace That Stays Quiet Until You Need It

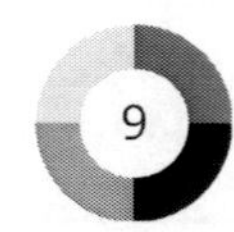

Traditional design software shows everything at once—icons, panels, hidden drawers. Canva takes a gentler approach: it reveals tools contextually, as you click. That means beginners can learn by doing, and experienced users aren't slowed by visual noise.

Here's the lay of the land, in plain language you will remember:

- **Left Sidebar:** your library. Templates, Projects, Brand, Folders, and Apps live here. Think of it as a well-labeled cupboard.
- **Top Search:** your radar. Type what you want—"Instagram carousel," "A4 flyer," "modern resume"—and jump straight to relevant formats.
- **Top Menu**: your global controls—undo/redo, file actions, resize (inside a design), version history.
- **Canvas (center):** where your design happens.
- **Contextual Toolbar**: appears when you select text, images, or shapes. It changes based on what you've clicked, keeping the interface calm.

What matters most is not memorizing names—it's forming a mental map. After a few sessions, your hand will move to the sidebar without thinking. That's when design speeds up: not because you rush, but because clutter disappears and decisions get clearer.

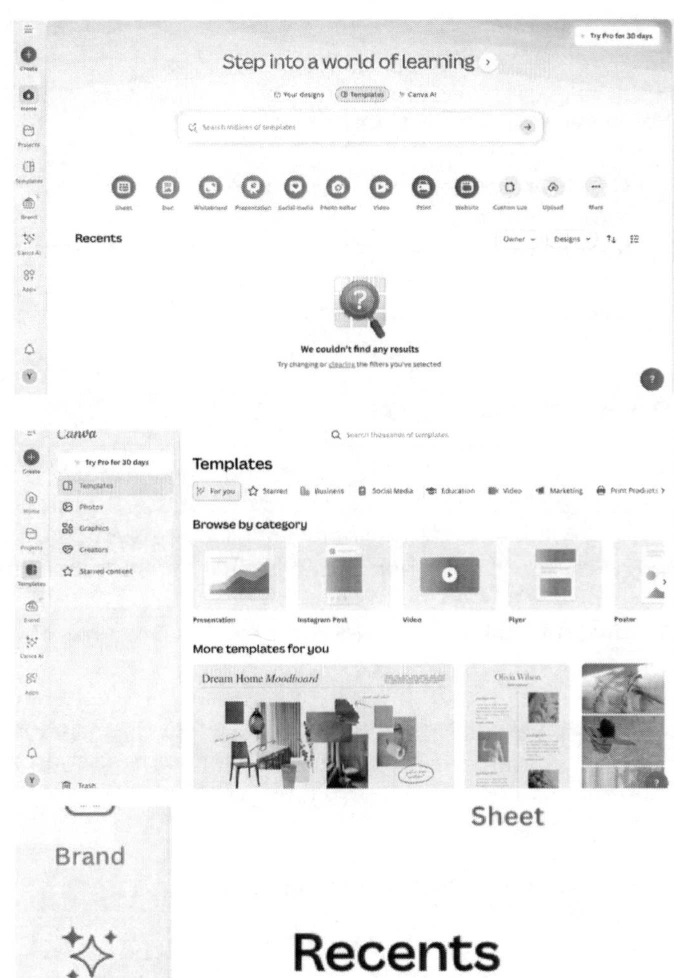

Attention — The "Click Wander" Trap. When you don't know where to look, you click everywhere. Pause for ten seconds instead. Ask: "What am I editing—text, an image, or the layout?" Then click the object first. The right toolbar will appear, every time.

Real Scenario — The Surprise Teacher. A non-designer opened a template and clicked on a headline by accident. The font toolbar appeared with size, weight, spacing. "Oh," she said, "it tells me what to do." Exactly. Canva teaches by showing only the tools you need in the moment.

Mini Exercise — A Three-Minute Tour

Log in. Open a design (any format).

1. Click a text box → notice the font controls.
2. Click an image → notice crop, flip, adjust.
3. Click outside everything → the toolbar vanishes.
4. Write this note: "When I select X, Canva shows Y." That sentence builds your mental model.

The Dashboard: Your Control Room (and Time Saver)

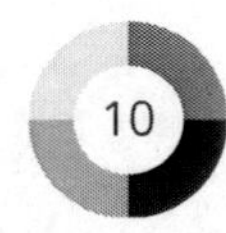

The dashboard is not a hallway to rush through—it's the room where you plan your day. Treat it well, and future-you will move at twice the speed. That's why you need to organize it well now for a quicker search later.

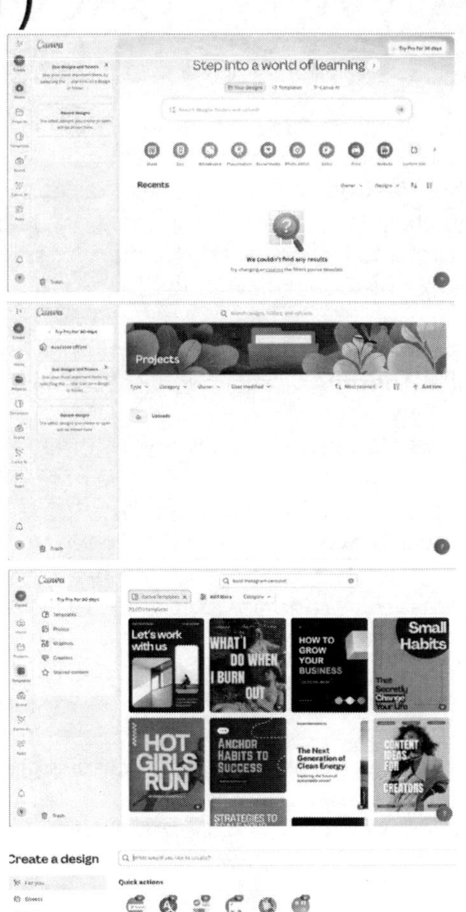

You'll see four zones that matter:

1. **Create a design —** the big purple button that picks your format and size.
2. **Recent projects** — autosaved designs you touched last.
3. **Folders** — your structure; absolutely worth five minutes now.
4. **Recommended templates** — suggestions that get smarter as Canva learns what you make.

Dashboard and Projects

Start by creating two folders: Personal and Work/School. Almost every design you make belongs to one of these. Later, you can add subfolders (e.g., Personal → Social Posts, Work → Client A). Organization is not a personality trait; it's a workflow multiplier.

Common Pitfall — The "Recent Projects Graveyard"

New users let everything pile up in Recent Projects. After a few weeks, they scroll for minutes to find a file. That friction kills momentum. Move finished drafts into folders as soon as you stop working on them—even if you plan to return tomorrow. The habit is the point.

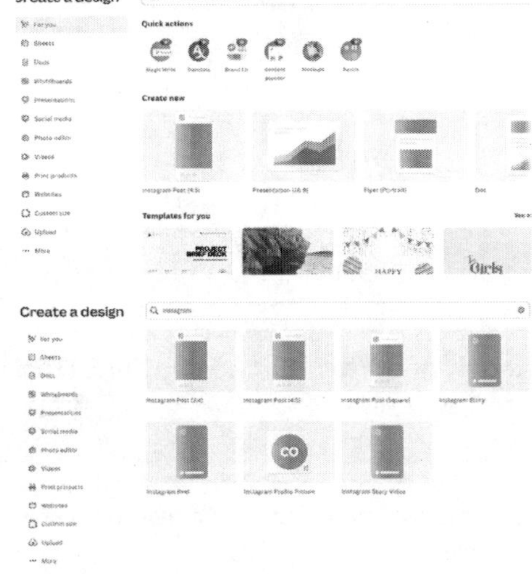

Real Scenario — Saving an Hour a Week

A freelancer had 120 designs floating in Recent. We built a quick structure: Clients, Marketing, Templates, Archive. Searching dropped from minutes to seconds. Over a year, that adds up to days of time reclaimed.

Pro Tip — Pin Your Active Files

If you work on three assets this week (say, a carousel, a slide deck, a flyer), add a "★ Active" folder. Pin it to the top. Move files out when they ship. You'll focus faster when your current work is always visible.

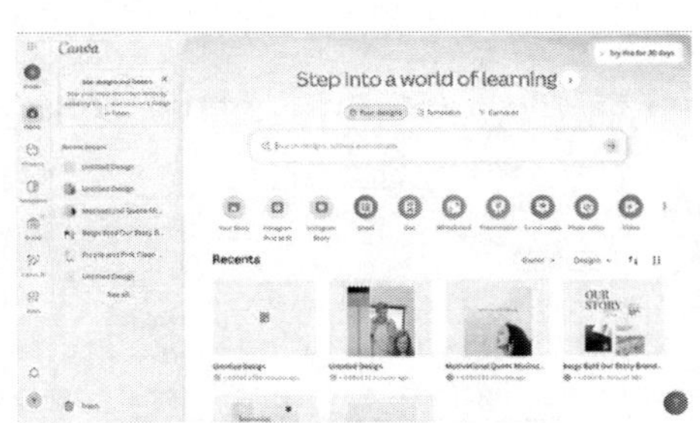

Mini Exercise — Two Folders, One Rule

Create Personal and Work/School. Move your practice design into one. Write a tiny rule under each:

- Personal → Anything for me (social, hobby, study).
- Work/School → Anything shared with others (client, team, teacher).
- Small rules reduce decision fatigue later.

Finding and Using Templates: From Blank to Branded

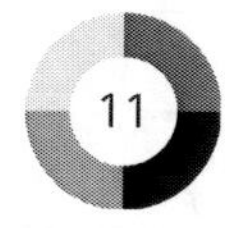

Templates are Canva's superpower. They remove blank-page anxiety and give you immediate structure—hierarchy, spacing, and rhythm you can study while you customize. But a template is scaffolding, not a finished building. Your job is to adapt it until it speaks in your voice.

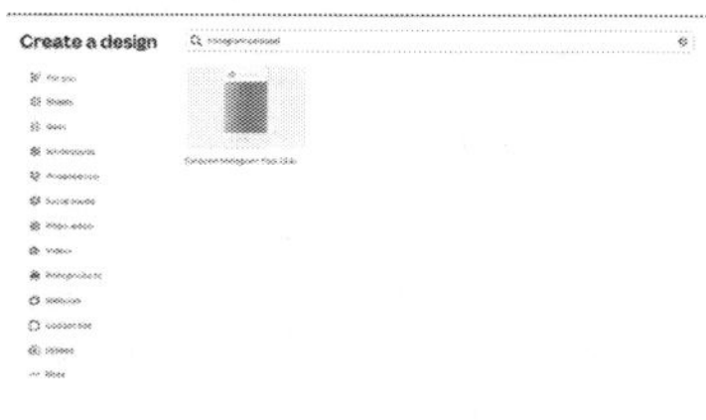

Start with intent. Type what you actually need into the search bar: "minimal pitch deck," **"bold Instagram carousel,"** "A4 price list," "modern resume." Then apply filters—style (minimal/modern/elegant), color, and orientation. Narrowing options keeps your attention on quality rather than quantity.

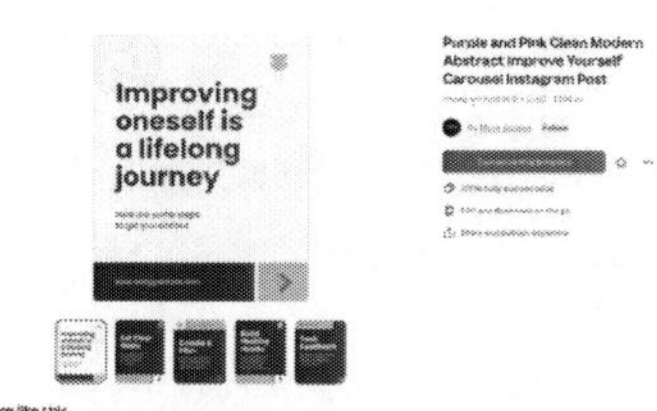

Open three candidates and read them like a designer:

- **Hierarchy**: can you tell what's most important at a glance?
- **Spacing**: do the margins and gaps feel generous enough to breathe?
- **Readability**: are the font sizes and contrasts comfortable on a phone screen?

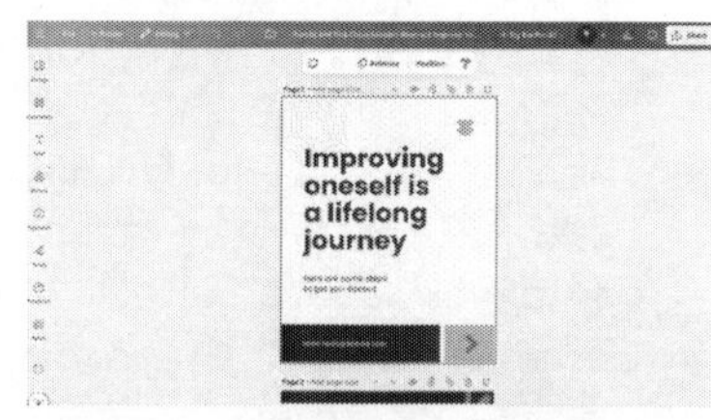

Pick your favorite and begin owning it. Change a palette color to match your taste, replace the hero image with something relevant, adjust the heading font weight if the default is too delicate or too heavy. Customize at least three elements (color, imagery, typography). This breaks the "I've seen this template before" feeling and moves the design into your world.

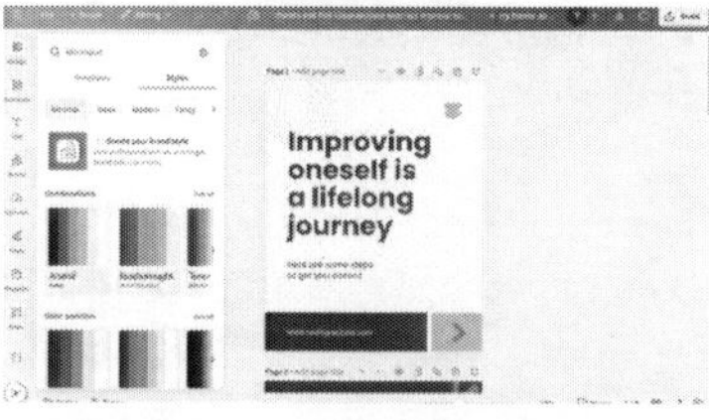

Attention — Don't Over-Edit All at Once
Change one variable at a time. First palette, then fonts, then images. If the design gets worse, undo the last change and try a different adjustment. Good design is often a sequence of small, reversible moves.

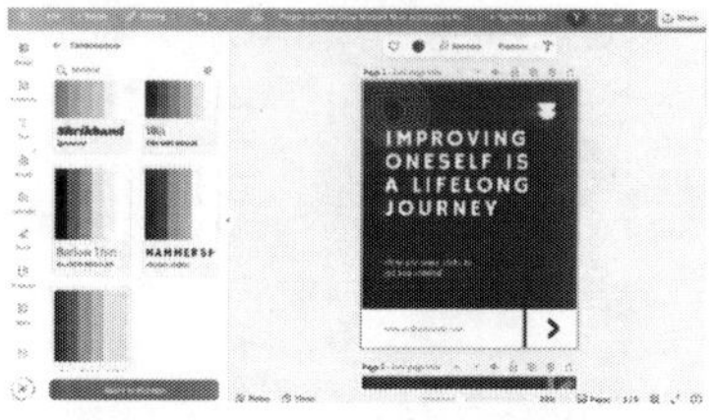

Real Scenario — The Quiet Upgrade
A bakery owner used a bright, playful template for a weekly specials post. It didn't match her cozy brand. We muted the palette, swapped the geometric font for a warm serif, and replaced stock sprinkles with her own croissant photo. Same layout, new voice. Customers noticed—and orders rose.

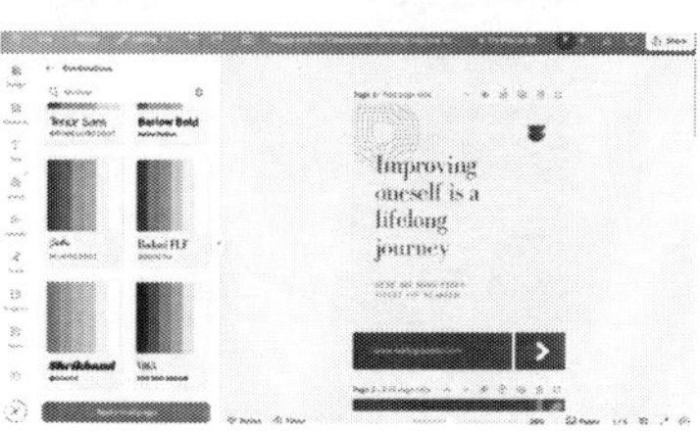

Pro Tip — Build a "Taste Board"
Create a single page with 5–6 swatches (your likely colors), 2 heading fonts, 2 body fonts, and 6–8 example images that feel on-brand. Keep it open while you customize templates. It's easier to adapt when your taste is visible.

Mini Exercise — Your First Owned Template

Search for "Instagram carousel."

1. Apply the Minimalist style filter and pick a set with clear margins.
2. Change the palette to two colors you love (plus black/white).
3. Replace the hero image on slide 1 with one of your photos.
4. Adjust the H1 size until it feels easy to read on a phone (aim for large and clean).
5. Export slide 1 as PNG and view it on your phone. Ask: "Would I pause to read this?" If not, increase contrast or simplify the text.

Recap — The First Milestone, Locked In

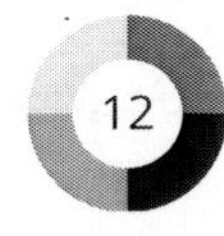

A quick recap solidifies new knowledge. The point is not to tick boxes; it's to feel how much smoother things already are.

- You have a single account that autosaves across devices.
- You can describe the interface in your own words and predict where tools will appear.
- Your dashboard now has the beginnings of a structure, so files don't disappear into "Recent."
- And you've taken a template from generic to personal by changing palette, fonts, and imagery.

Those are professional habits. Keep them, and every future chapter will feel easier.

Common Mistakes — Not Failures, Just Fixable Frictions

- Beginners don't ruin designs; they usually slow them down with avoidable friction. Here are the usual suspects and the antidotes that restore flow.
- Two Accounts, Two Worlds. If you've signed up with both email and Google, pick one and migrate. Share designs from the "old" account to the "new" one, then stop using the duplicate. Simplicity is speed.
- The Dashboard Pile-Up. When everything lives in Recent, scrolling becomes your daily exercise. Create Personal and Work/School now. Move anything older than two weeks into a subfolder called Archive. You can always search later.
- Copying Without Customizing. Templates are not your brand. Change at least three variables—color, typography, imagery—before you export. It's the difference between "nice template" and "your voice."
- Endless Scrolling, No Filters. The library is massive; your time isn't. Search with intent ("minimal investor deck," not just "presentation") and apply filters. Decision fatigue drops and quality rises.

"Do It Now" Homework — 20 Minutes That Change Your Next Week

End each major section with action, so learning sticks.

1. **Account + Naming.** Confirm your login method. Create a tiny text file pinned to your desktop: Canva — Naming Rules. Add your chosen pattern (e.g., YYYY-MM Project — Short Title — v01).
2. **Interface Tour.** Open a template and click text, image, and shape in turn. Write one sentence in your notebook: "When I select X, Canva shows Y."
3. **Dashboard Setup.** Create Personal and Work/School folders. Add a ★ to an Active folder and pin it to the top. Move your current file there.
4. **Owned Template**. Search, filter, like, save, start customizing. Change palette, headline font, and main image. Export slide 1 as PNG and review it on your phone. Tweak contrast if needed.

QR Bonus (end of module hub): First 60 Minutes Checklist + 10 Starter Templates + Dimensions & Export Table. Scan to duplicate the templates directly and print the checklist if you like working on paper.

Closing Thought

You've stepped from curiosity into practice. You now have a reliable account, a mental map of the interface, a dashboard that will scale with your work, and your first customized design.

The software didn't change—you did. In Chapter 2, we'll shape your eye so your designs read clearly at a glance. Good typography and honest contrast are quiet superpowers. You're ready for them.

Chapter 2

Typography & Color Made Simple: Clarity, Style & Visual Impact

Chapter 2

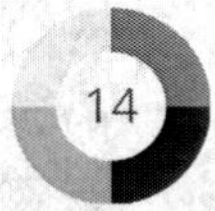

Typography & Color Made Simple: Clarity, Style & Visual Impact

Open any feed, slide deck, brochure, or landing page and notice what your brain does first: it doesn't read. It scans. It takes in big shapes, relative sizes, bolds versus regulars, darks on lights, and the temperature of color. In milliseconds, it decides: this looks trustworthy / this looks messy; this feels premium / this feels cheap; this is worth my time / this is noise. Typography and color are the two levers that drive those snap judgments. They are not decoration. They are the skeleton and blood of your message. **So, before they read your words, they read your design.**

Canva's promise is speed—and speed is a gift only if it comes with control. Click too quickly and you fall into the "font buffet" (six styles in the same design) or the "rainbow palette" (every hue shouting at once). That's how good ideas get dismissed as amateur. On the other hand, when you master hierarchy (what the eye sees first), pairing (which fonts sing together), palette (which colors feel like a brand), and contrast (whether people can actually read), your work stops looking like a template and starts reading like a brand.

This chapter slows you down—on purpose. We'll learn to stage a headline like a headline (commanding, spacious); to cast the right supporting font beside it (calm, legible); to assemble three or four colors that live well together across social, print, and slides; and to pressure-test every combination on the device that matters most: a phone. By the end, you won't be asking, "Which font looks nice?" You'll be asking, "Which hierarchy gets my idea read in three seconds?" You'll stop dabbling with colors and start carrying a palette that makes your work recognizable at a glance.

Promise: the techniques here are simple, repeatable, and visible. Apply them once and you'll feel the difference; apply them for a month and others will feel the difference in you.

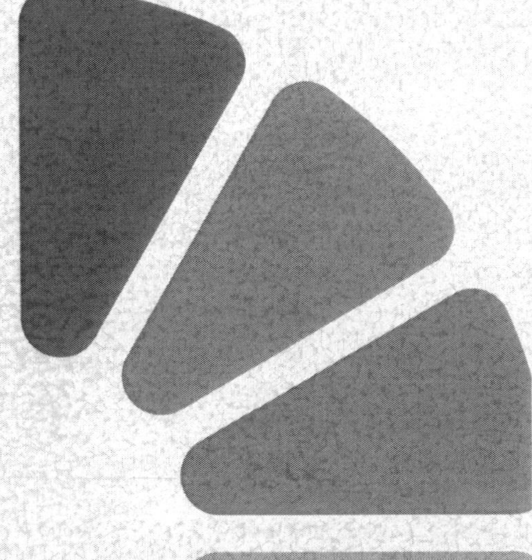

What You'll Do in 10 Minutes (and why it matters)

A small, focused sprint turns theory into muscle memory.

1. Set the stage (1 min).
2. Create a 1080×1350 (portrait) design in Canva—phone-first, so decisions are honest.
3. Build a three-step hierarchy (3 min).
4. Add three text boxes: Headline (largest, bold), Subhead (medium, regular), Body (small, regular). Place them with generous spacing.
5. Pick a proven pairing (3 min).
6. Set the Headline to a confident serif (e.g., Playfair Display or Merriweather). Set Subhead + Body to a clean sans (e.g., Inter, Open Sans, Montserrat). Already, you're 70% professional.
7. Load a 3–4 color palette (2 min).
8. From Canva's Color styles, choose: Primary (background), Secondary (headline), Accent (buttons/markers), Neutral (body text). Save to Brand Kit if available.
9. Make it readable (1 min).
10. Test contrast: white on navy; charcoal on pale beige. Preview on your phone. If you squint, it still reads? Good.

That one canvas now demonstrates hierarchy, pairing, palette, and contrast—the four decisions you'll refine for the rest of the chapter.

Section 1 — Hierarchy: The Map That Gets Your Message Read

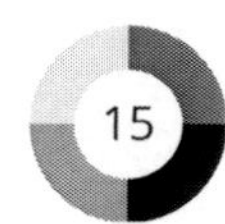

Why it matters.

If everything speaks at the same volume, nothing is heard. Hierarchy is how you assign roles: the headline grabs, the subhead frames, the body explains, the CTA directs. Done right, your design reads itself in the viewer's mind before they consciously read it.

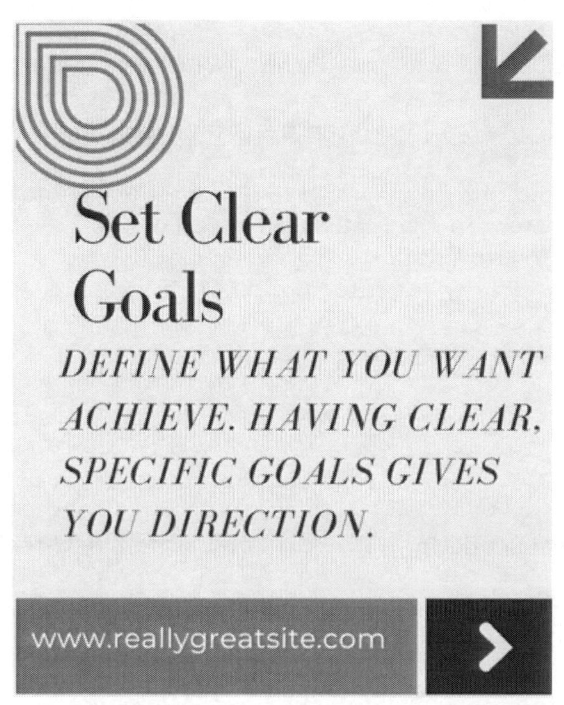

How to structure hierarchy in Canva (with intent).

- **Size**: Let the headline be decisively larger. Think 2.2–3× the body size for social, 1.6–2× for print.
- **Weight**: Bold for headlines, regular for body. Use italics sparingly (emphasis, not style).
- **Spacing**: Give each level breathing room. Tight spacing cheapens; air sells.
- **Position**: The eye lands high-left on Western layouts. Use that to your advantage.
- **Color**: One decisive color for the headline, then calm neutrals for body.

Real Scenario — "The Poster No One Read."

A community workshop poster placed date, title, and venue in the same size. People stared and kept walking. We rebuilt it: giant event name; medium-sized date/venue; small, crisp details. Same words, different ladder. Turnout doubled.

Pro Tip — The Three-Second Test.

Shrink your design to phone-thumbnail size in Canva's zoom. Can you grasp the headline (and only the headline) in three seconds? If not, increase size/weight and clear more space around it.

Mini Exercise — Ladder of Meaning.

Duplicate your 10-minute design into three copies.

A) Keep all sizes close (bad on purpose).
B) Make the headline 2.5× body, subhead 1.6× body.
C) Keep B's sizes but add more padding/space between levels.

Preview all on your phone. Which one feels most confident? That's the effect of hierarchy.

Section 2 — Font Pairing: Two Voices, One Message

Why it matters.

Fonts carry personality: serifs often read as editorial, premium, or classic; sans serifs read as modern, clean, or tech-forward; scripts whisper human warmth but can overwhelm legibility. The aim is to set two voices that harmonize—never competing solos.

Reliable pairings (start here, then evolve).

- **Editorial authority**: Merriweather (H1) + Inter (body).
- **Modern product:** Montserrat (H1) + Source Sans Pro (body).
- **Warm boutique**: Playfair Display (H1) + Lato (body).
- **Friendly educator**: Poppins (H1) + Noto Sans (body).

Rules that keep you safe.

- Cap yourself at 2 fonts (3 only if one is a tiny accent, like numerals or a script signature).
- Contrast, don't clash: pair categories (serif + sans). Avoid two loud display fonts together.
- Be consistent across assets: same pair on posts, decks, brochures. Repetition builds brand memory.

Real Scenario — The "Six Fonts, One Site" Freelance Portfolio.

Talented work, but the site felt chaotic. We cut to two: a dignified serif for headlines and a neutral sans for long reads. Inquiries rose the same month—not because the work improved, but because trust did.

Attention — Readability Across Weights.

Some sans look beautiful at 400 weight but fall apart at 700; some serifs are elegant in H1 but muddy in small sizes. Always test your exact sizes on phone.

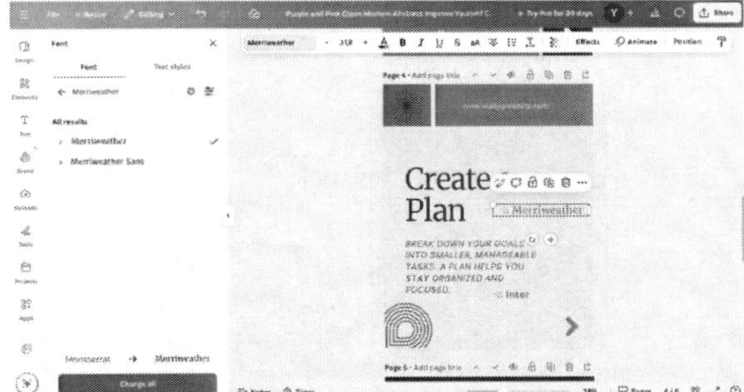

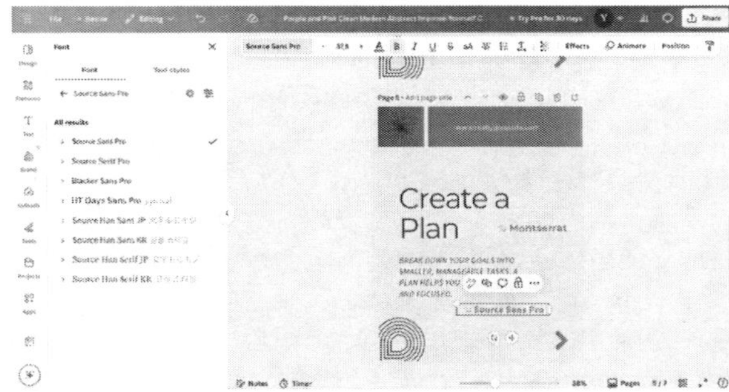

Pro Tip — Numerals Matter.

If your brand communicates numbers (pricing, metrics), compare numeral shapes. Pick the font with clean, unambiguous digits. It silently improves professionalism.

Mini Exercise — The Pairing Bake-Off.

Create one layout. Duplicate it four times, testing the four pairings above. Export a PDF with all five pages. Share with a friend or team and ask only: "Which version feels most us?" Choose by feel and legibility.

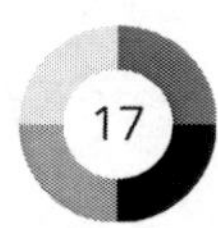

Section 3 — Palettes: Three or Four Colors That Behave Like a Brand

Why it matters.

Color sets mood instantly and creates memory over time. Chaotic color choices lead to forgettable brands; disciplined palettes lead to recognition. The best palettes are small, deliberate, and versatile.

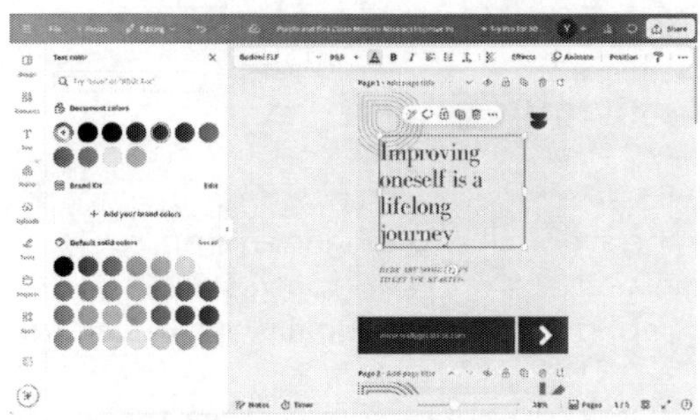

A simple, durable palette structure.

- Primary (60%) — background or dominant blocks (e.g., navy).
- Secondary (30%) — headline or key highlights (e.g., teal).
- Accent (10%) — buttons, bullets, small emphasis (e.g., coral).
- Neutrals — white/near-white and charcoal/near-black for text.

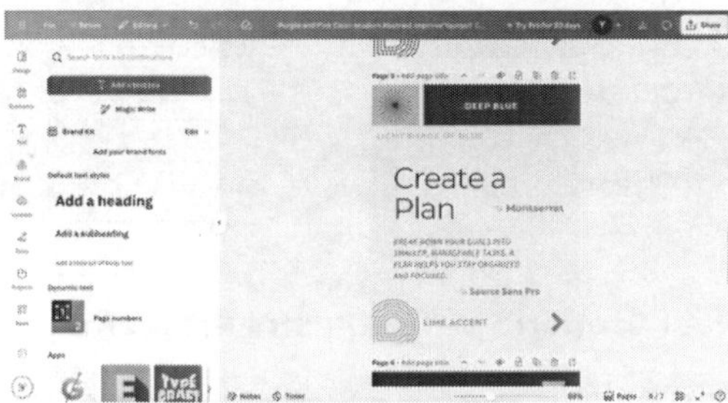

Where to find or build palettes in Canva.

- Extract from Image: drop in a brand photo; save the suggested swatches.
- Color Wheel / Styles: search "calm," "bold," "vintage" to find curated sets.
- Brand Kit: lock your final four and stop experimenting every post.

Real Scenario — The Startup With Five Lives.

This creator's grid swung weekly: lavender, then orange, then mint, then red. Nothing stuck. We committed to deep blue + light slate + lime accent. Three weeks later, people started saying, "I recognized your post before I saw the handle."

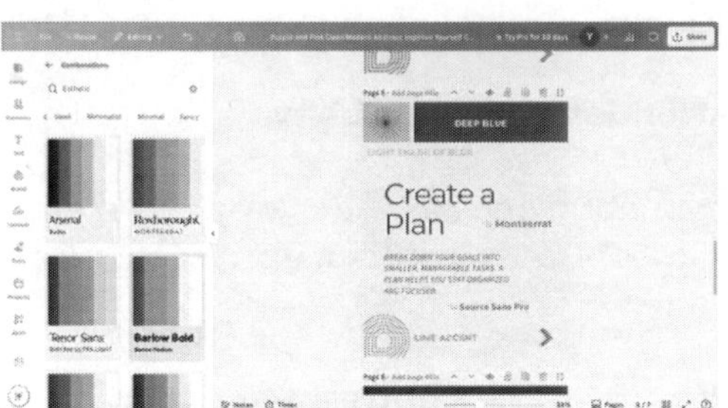

Pro Tip — Temperature & Contrast.

- Choose a base temperature (cool → trust, warm → energy) and keep contrast workable. Pale text on pale backgrounds will not survive mobile feeds.
- Alternative Fast Track — Monochrome + Accent.
- Pick one hue (e.g., blue) and live in its shades (navy, sky, slate). Add one pop accent (e.g., coral) for CTAs. Easy to manage, hard to mess up.

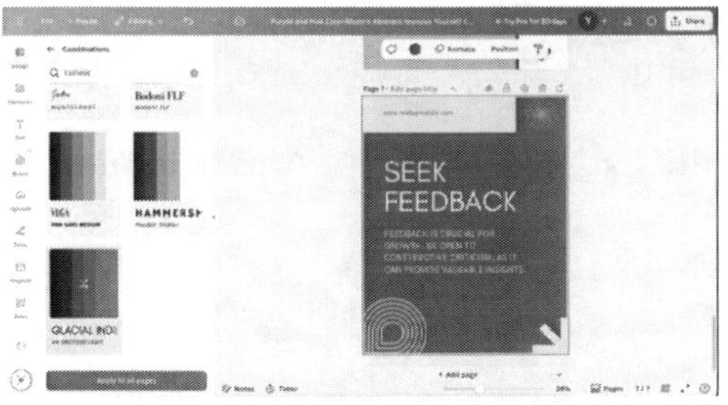

Mini Exercise — Palette in the Wild.

Search your camera roll for one photo that feels like your vibe (studio corner, product flatlay, city dusk). Use "Extract Palette" in Canva. Save those four colors to Brand Kit and apply them to a two-slide design. That's your first brand board.

Section 4 — Contrast: Legibility Is a Promise, Not a Preference

Why it matters.

If it isn't readable, it isn't communication. Low contrast is the silent killer of engagement: lovely aesthetic, zero comprehension. High contrast isn't about harshness; it's about clarity. **Practical ways to secure readability:**

- Dark on light or light on dark for body text. Avoid mid-tone on mid-tone.
- Overlays: place text over busy photos using a 30–60% translucent rectangle or gradient.
- Shadow/Outline with restraint: a 1–2 px text outline can rescue edge cases—but don't rely on it as a style.
- Phone preview: always, always check at hand-held size.

Real Scenario — The Pastel Problem.

A wellness brand loved pale sage on cream. Beautiful in the art board, invisible in Stories. We kept the vibe but flipped roles: charcoal text on sage blocks, sage accents around it. Same mood, new clarity.

Attention — Accessibility.

If your audience includes readers on dim screens or outdoors, push contrast up. It's inclusive and it converts better.

Pro Tip — CTA Contrast Multiplier.

CTAs need contrast in three ways: color (button vs background), weight (bold vs regular), and spacing (air around it). Treat the CTA like a mini headline; let it breathe.

Mini Exercise — The Contrast Ladder.

Create a 3×3 grid of small CTA buttons.

- Row 1: low-contrast combos.
- Row 2: medium.
- Row 3: high-contrast.
- Preview on phone in bright light. Which row survives? Make that your new baseline.

Section 5 — Putting It Together (With Reasoning, Not Only Rules)

Let's design a simple promo tile you could actually ship today—and explain why each choice works.

1. **Canvas**: 1080×1350 portrait (IG feed and LinkedIn-friendly). Phone-first reality.
2. **Hierarchy**: "Free Workshop: Build Your First Portfolio" as the H1. It's the job of the headline to earn the rest of the read. Make it large, bold, and short.
3. **Pairing**: Merriweather (H1) + Inter (body). Editorial authority + system clarity.
4. **Palette**: Navy background, off-white body text, teal subheads, coral CTA. Cool trust + one warm spark.
5. **Contrast**: White-on-navy for H1; charcoal-on-pale slate for body. No guessing.
6. **CTA**: "Save Your Seat →" in coral, bold, with comfortable padding.
7. **Spacing**: Bigger than you think. White space equals confidence.
8. **Consistency**: Save this as "Promo — Master Template." Duplicate for future workshops, swap only title/date.

Result: clear ladder of attention, two voices in harmony, a palette you can reuse, and legibility that survives a shaky bus ride.

Checklist — Typography & Color Locked

1. **Hierarchy** reads at a glance. **When you zoom out**—or hold your phone at arm's length—you can still identify the headline instantly, then the subhead, then the body. You no longer hope people read; you guide how they read.
2. **Two fonts,** one voice. Your chosen **pair** handles everything: headlines feel distinctive, body stays effortless, numerals look clean. Across posts, slides, and PDFs, the text feels like the same brand speaking in different rooms.
3. A **palette** you can live with. **Three or four colors r**ecur across assets without strain. Primary dominates, secondary supports, accent sparks action, neutrals carry text. Your grid begins to look like you, not like "whatever was cute today."
4. **Contrast** that respects readers and contexts. **Headlines and CTAs** are unmistakable; paragraphs don't fade; overlays come out when photos get busy. You've traded fragile aesthetics for durable clarity—especially on mobile.

When all four are true, your designs stop asking for attention and start earning it.

Common Mistakes — And How to Correct Them (for real-world freelancers & teams)

Mistake 1: The Font Parade.

- Six fonts, three scripts, every weight. It looks like indecision, which feels like inexperience.
- Fix: cap yourself at two (serif + sans). Save the pair to Brand Kit. Refuse "just one more" unless there's a functional reason.

Mistake 2: Mood Swings in Color.

- Every post a new palette. It might feel creative; it reads as unstable.
- Fix: adopt a 60-30-10 palette. If you're bored, vary layout, photography, or texture—not the base colors.

Mistake 3: Pretty but Illegible.

- Low-contrast aesthetics that die on phones.
- Fix: commit to readability. Use overlays, raise contrast, and test on mobile in sunlight. Beauty that can't be read doesn't sell.

Mistake 4: Flat Pages, Flat Sales.

- Equal sizes and weights, no visual path.
- Fix: make the headline decisively bigger, subhead supportive, body smaller with line-height tuned. Add air. Watch comprehension jump.

Why this matters.

None of these errors is fatal alone, but together they form an invisible wall of mistrust. Fix them, and clients see "professional" before they've processed a single sentence.

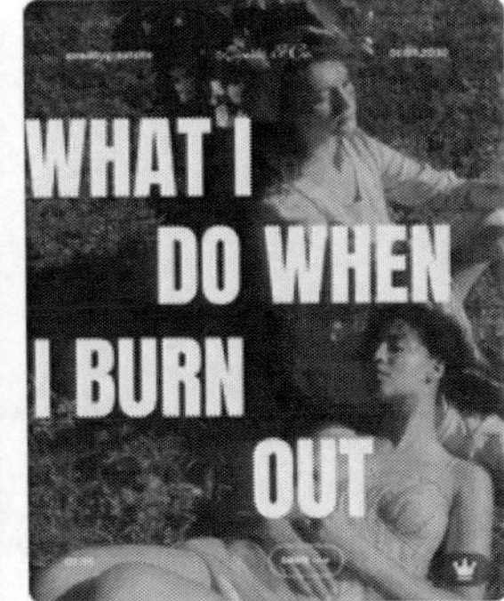

"Do It Now" Homework — 90 Minutes of Design That Sticks

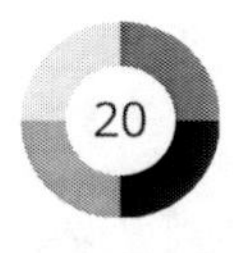

1) Hierarchy Audit (20 min).
Open three past designs. Without changing words, rebuild the hierarchy: enlarge H1 dramatically, clarify subheads, add space. Export before/after. Note what changed in your gut reaction.

2) Pairing Decision (20 min).
Choose your long-term pair (serif + sans). Apply to: one IG post, one slide, one one-pager. Save to Brand Kit so future-you doesn't re-decide every time.

3) Palette Build (25 min).
Extract from a photo or pick a curated set. Lock Primary/Secondary/Accent/Neutrals. Create a one-page "Brand Board" with swatches, font pair, buttons, and a sample headline.

4) Contrast Stress Test (25 min).
Design a CTA block in three contrasts: low, mid, high. Export and test on your phone under bright light. Choose the one that survives the worst conditions. Make it your default.

Outcome: a practical typography + color system that speeds every future decision.

Closing Thought

Type and color look like cosmetics from a distance. Up close, they're governance. They create order without asking permission; they teach the eye where to go and how to feel. With a sturdy hierarchy, a faithful font pair, a palette you can live with, and contrast you can trust, you won't merely make "prettier" things—you'll make clearer ones. And clarity is the most generous thing you can give your audience. Next, we'll translate this clarity into structure on the canvas—grids, alignment, grouping, and placement—so that your pages not only speak well, they hold together under pressure.

Chapter 3

Layout Essentials: Structure, Balance & Smart Positioning

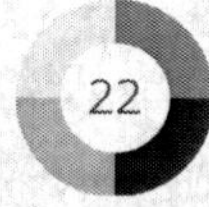

Chapter 3

Layout Essentials: Structure, Balance & Smart Positioning

A design can have beautiful colors, striking images, and clever text—and still feel wrong. The problem is often invisible: the layout. When elements float without connection, when text is misaligned, or when spacing is inconsistent, the viewer feels unease without knowing why. Good layout, on the other hand, is quiet and confident. It guides the eye naturally from headline to image to call-to-action.

In Canva, mastering layout is about learning how to place elements with intention. This chapter is not about decoration—it's about structure. Imagine building a house: typography and color are your paint and furniture, but the layout is the architecture. Without it, the whole thing collapses.

By the end of this chapter, you will know how to:

- Use grids to anchor your elements so they stay balanced.
- Apply alignment tools that make your text and images snap into place.
- Group elements so you can move, resize, or duplicate entire sections at once.
- Master layering and positioning, deciding what stays in front, what sits behind, and how depth creates focus.

This is where your work begins to look "professional." Most beginners struggle not because of creativity, but because of spacing and alignment. Once you fix that, your designs instantly look more polished—without changing a single font or color.

What You'll Do in 10 Minutes (and why it matters)

- Explore Canva's grid system and drop a few elements into place.
- Practice aligning text and shapes with the smart guides.
- Group two or more objects and move them together.
- Layer an image behind text and adjust transparency for balance.

These may sound simple, but they are the backbone of every design you will ever create.

Grids: The Hidden Skeleton of Every Layout

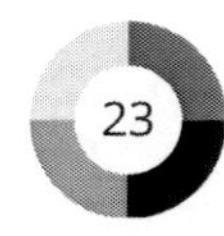

Grids are invisible lines that organize content. Newspapers, websites, posters—all of them rely on grids. Canva offers a range of preset grid layouts (one column, two-column split, thirds, quarters) that help even beginners achieve professional spacing without measuring pixels.

To use grids:

1. From the sidebar, open Elements → Grids.
2. Drag a grid style onto your canvas.
3. Drop images or shapes into the grid slots—they'll automatically resize to fit.

The beauty of grids is consistency. Instead of guessing where to place a photo, you know it will always align. That frees your mind to focus on the message, not the math.

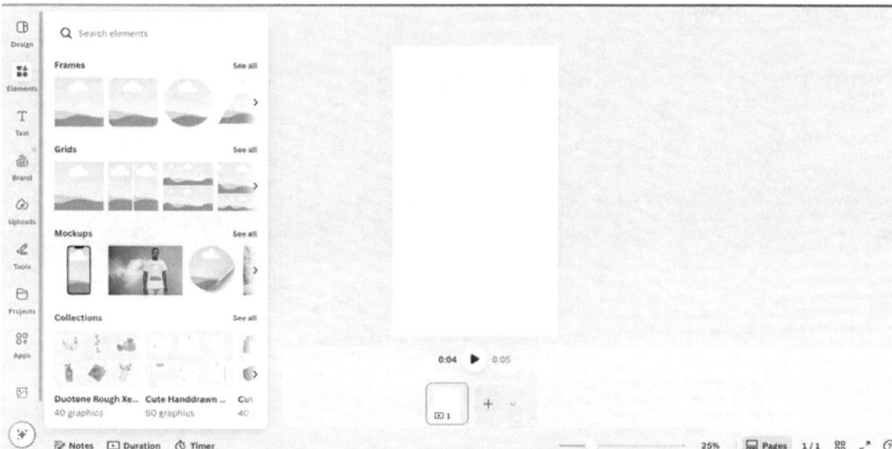

Real Scenario — Instagram Carousel That Feels Cohesive

A fitness coach wanted to post a 5-slide carousel of workout tips. Without grids, each slide looked slightly different—margins uneven, images cropped awkwardly. With a simple 2-column grid, every slide suddenly matched. The message felt cohesive, and engagement doubled.

Pro Tip — Break the Grid Intentionally

Rules matter until you're skilled enough to bend them. Use grids to anchor most elements, then allow one photo or headline to break the structure. That contrast draws attention.

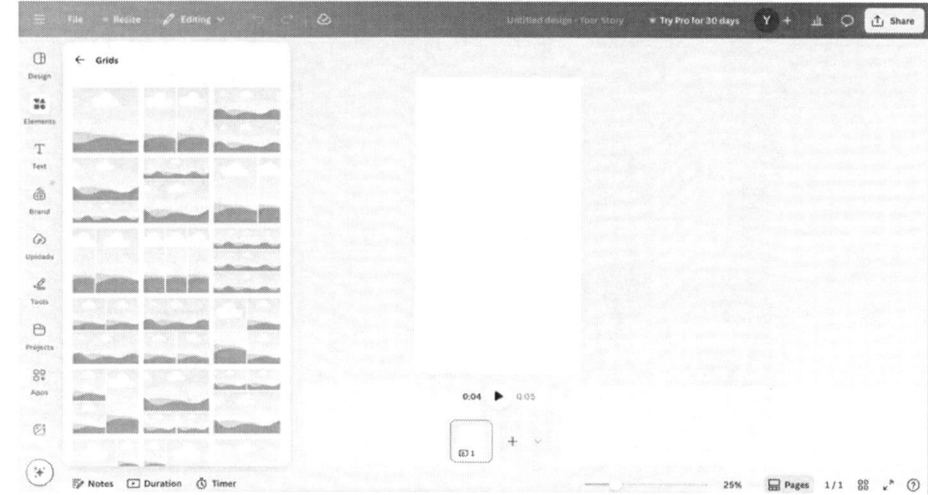

Mini Exercise

Open a blank Instagram Post (1080×1080). Insert a 2-column grid. Drop two photos inside. Then replace one photo with a colored background and text overlay. Export and look at it on your phone. Notice how balanced it feels.

Alignment: Snapping Into Place

Alignment is the invisible glue that holds design together. Canva's smart guides make it almost impossible to misalign—if you pay attention. When you drag an element, pink lines appear showing center points, edges, or equal spacing with other objects.

Why alignment matters:

- **Legibility**: aligned text is easier to read.
- **Professionalism**: aligned images show attention to detail.
- **Harmony**: aligned objects feel calmer and more intentional.

To practice alignment:

1. Add three text boxes.
2. Drag them until the pink lines show equal spacing.
3. Select them all, then use the "Align top" or "Align middle" options in the toolbar.

Common Pitfall — Eyeballing Alignment

Many beginners "eyeball" placements, thinking it looks fine. But one pixel off is visible on a phone screen. Trust Canva's guides—they exist for a reason.

Real Scenario — Pitch Deck Slide

A startup founder once showed investors a slide where bullet points were slightly staggered. The content was strong, but the visual chaos undermined credibility. After applying "Align left," the deck felt clean, sharp, and worthy of trust.

Mini Exercise

Create a flyer. Add a headline, subheadline, and call-to-action. Align all text boxes left. Then try aligning them center. Export both versions and compare: which looks calmer for your message?

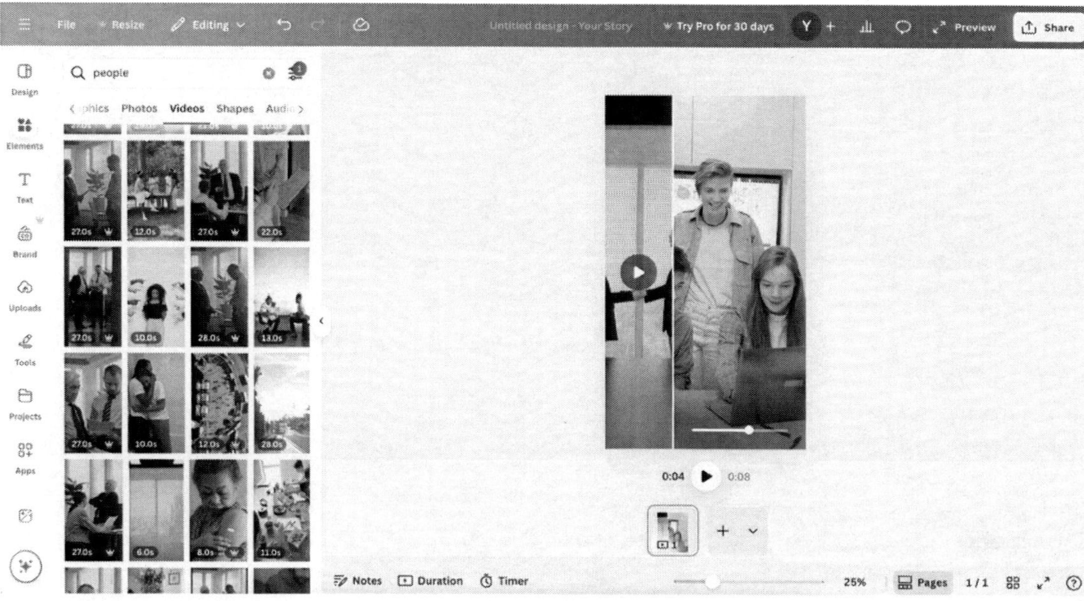

Grouping: Moving as One

Imagine trying to carry a stack of plates one by one. Grouping is like picking up the whole stack at once. In Canva, grouping lets you move or resize multiple elements together—headlines with subheads, icons with captions, photos with borders.

How to group:

1. Select multiple elements: Shift+click; Command+click (Apple) or drag across.
2. Click Group in the toolbar.
3. Now you can resize, duplicate, or move them as a unit.

Pro Tip — Use Grouping for Consistency

When you build a carousel, group the layout of one slide (image, text, button). Duplicate the grouped slide, then change the content. This keeps design consistent across slides.

Real Scenario — Event Flyer in Two Languages

A community organizer designed flyers in English and Spanish. By grouping the header, image, and CTA box, she could duplicate the entire layout and only replace the text. Both versions stayed identical in design—only the words changed.

Mini Exercise

Create a simple poster with a title, image, and button. Group them. Duplicate the group twice. Change the colors in each duplicate. Now you have three posters with identical structure but different moods.

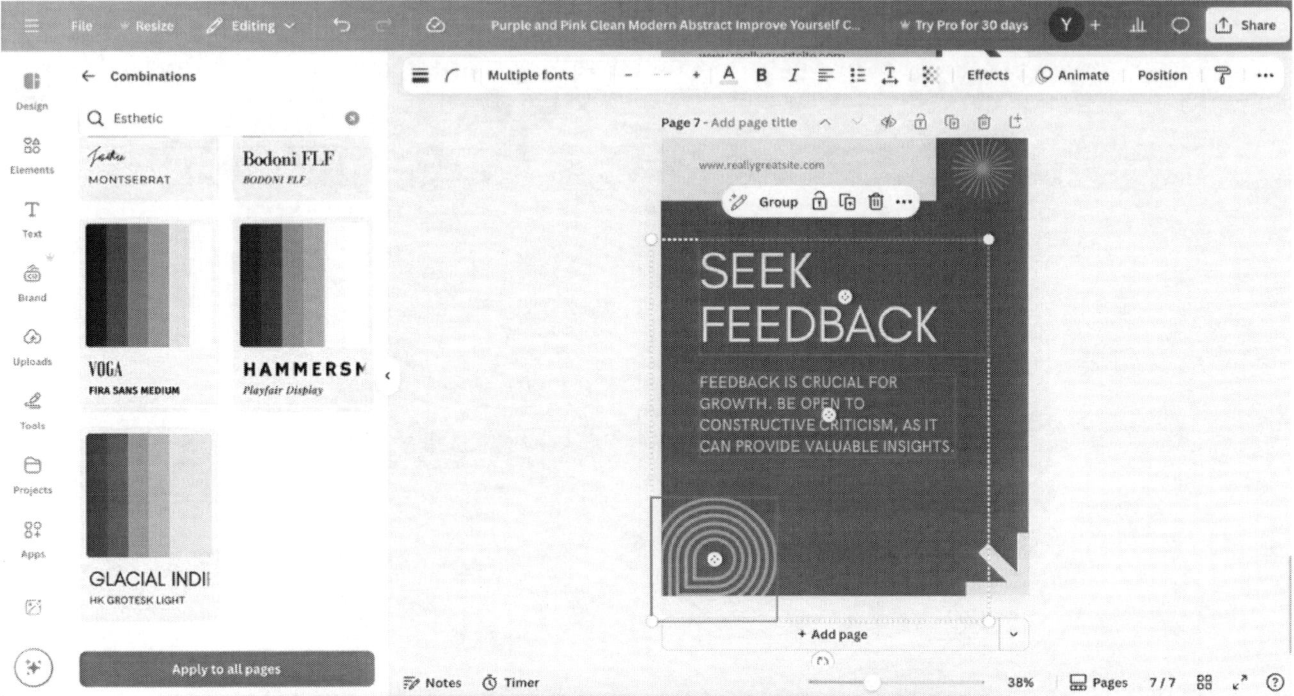

Positioning: Layers and Depth

Positioning determines what sits in front and what hides behind. Canva uses a simple layer stack, like sheets of paper. Every element you add goes on top by default. But you can send objects forward or backward to create depth.

Why it matters:

- Text should always sit above background images.
- Icons can overlap photos without hiding faces.
- Semi-transparent shapes can rest between background and text to improve readability.

How to use:

1. Right-click an element.
2. Choose "Arrange" backward or forward.
3. Adjust transparency if layering creates clutter.

Attention — Don't Overcrowd Layers

Too many overlapping shapes make a design heavy. Use layers with intention: one clear background, one focal image, one readable text area.

Real Scenario — YouTube Thumbnail That Pops

A gaming creator placed a character image behind bold text. The text was hard to read. We added a semi-transparent rectangle between them, adjusted transparency to 60%, and suddenly both text and character were visible. Click-through rates rose.

Mini Exercise

Create a social post. Add a background photo, a semi-transparent shape (rectangle at 60%), and bold text on top. Export and compare the readability with and without the shape.

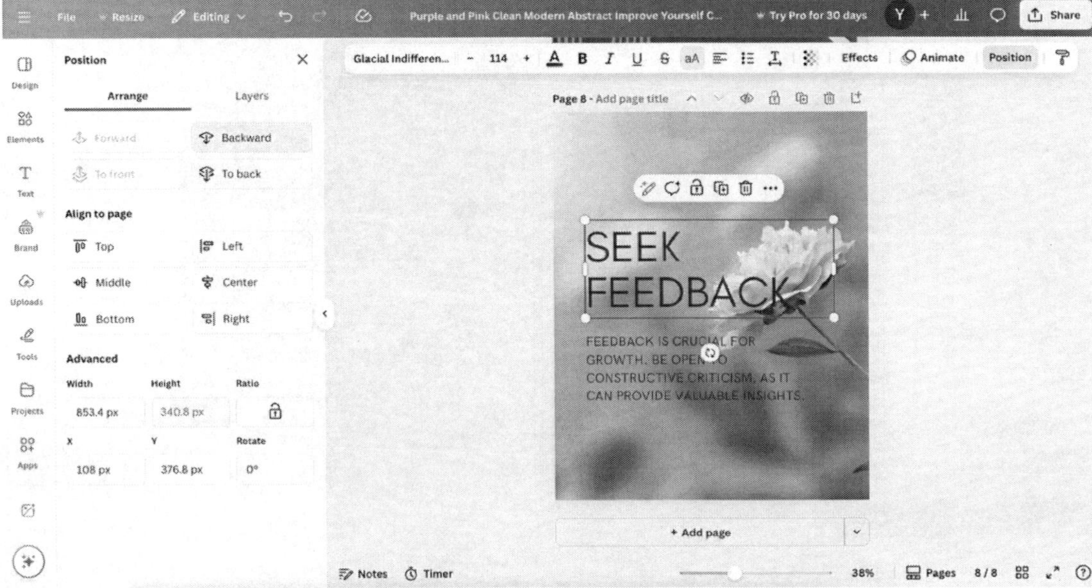

Checklist: Layout & Levels Locked In

Before moving on, confirm you can:

- Place images and text in grids for balance.
- Snap objects using alignment guides.
- Group elements to move or duplicate them together.
- Adjust layers to control depth and readability.

If these feel natural, your designs now have structure as well as style.

Common Mistakes — And Their Fixes

- Messy Spacing. Throwing objects randomly leads to chaotic layouts. Use grids as your training wheels until spacing feels natural.
- Ignoring Smart Guides. If you resist the pink lines, you're ignoring free help. Let Canva's guides do the math.
- Forgetting to Group. If you move text and image separately, they'll slip out of sync. Group and duplicate instead.
- Over-layering. Stacking too many shapes, images, and effects clutters the message. Keep depth intentional, not decorative.

Closing Thought

Mastering layout is like learning rhythm in music. Without it, even the best lyrics fall flat. With it, every design flows. By anchoring elements in grids, aligning them with guides, grouping logically, and layering with intention, you've crossed from "random" to "structured."

Next, we'll focus on Images & Elements—uploading, cropping, and using Canva's vast library to bring your designs to life.

Chapter 4

Working With Images & Elements: Clean Edits, Clarity & Control

Chapter 4

Working With Images & Elements: Clean Edits, Clarity & Control

Pictures carry the message—structure lets them speak. If layout is the architecture of your design, images are the windows that let light in. A single well-chosen photo can communicate mood, credibility, and context faster than a paragraph of text. **But images only work when they're handled well—imported at the right quality, framed with intention, layered with care, and stored in a system you can actually maintain.** This chapter is your guide to treating visuals like a professional: not as decorations, but as the core narrative components of your page.

We'll slow down and learn how images enter Canva (from your device, cloud drives, or Canva's built-in libraries), how to crop and frame them so the eye lands where you want, how to use transparency to balance text and background, and how to build a personal asset library that makes tomorrow faster than today. We'll also explore "elements"—icons, shapes, lines, frames—that quietly support your message.

Used well, these pieces reinforce hierarchy, rhythm, and clarity; used poorly, they add noise. By the end of this chapter, you'll move from "drag-and-drop" to directing the viewer's attention with purpose.

What You'll Do in 10 Minutes (and why it matters)

- A quick warm-up creates momentum and removes hesitation. In this short sprint you will:
- Upload one image from your device and one from Canva's stock library, so you can compare quality and style.
- Crop each image to a clear focal point and test a frame (circle or phone mockup) to see how it changes the story.
- Add a semi-transparent rectangle and place text on top, learning how transparency improves readability without killing the photo.
- Save both images to a Folder and Star them, so your asset library starts tidy and stays that way.

The point isn't to make something "perfect" yet—it's to feel how a few deliberate touches can turn a generic picture into a compelling, branded visual.

Uploads: Bringing Your World Into Canva

Why this matters.

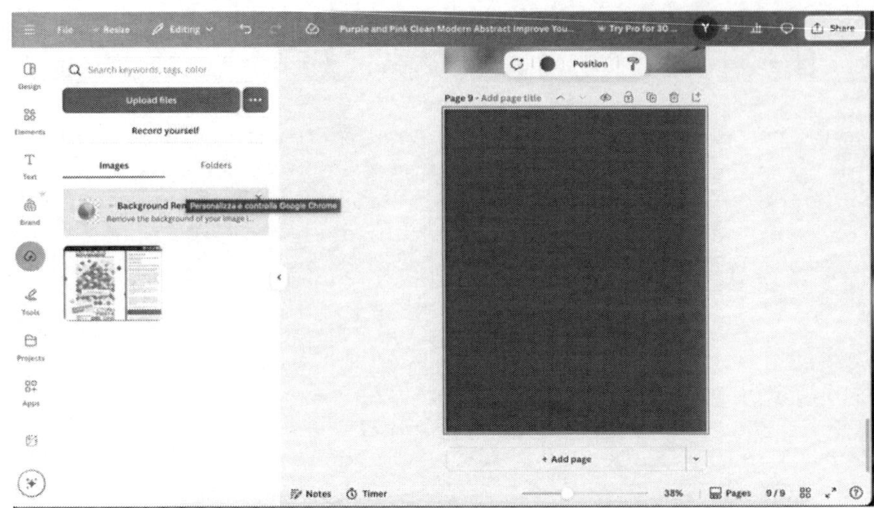

Every brand—personal or business—has a visual fingerprint: your environment, your products, your face, your city.

Uploading your own photos brings authenticity that stock cannot replicate. At the same time, Canva's built-in libraries are invaluable for filler images, conceptual shots, and quick experiments. You'll use both. The skill is choosing which source serves the message best.

How uploads work (with context).

- From any design, open the left sidebar and select Uploads.
- You can drag files in from your desktop or click Upload files to reach your computer, Google Drive, Dropbox, or Photos. Canva ingests common formats (JPG, PNG, SVG for vector icons, short MP4s/GIFs for motion), and it autosaves them to your account so you can reuse them later.

A few quality guardrails keep you out of trouble:

- **Resolution**: For social, aim for the design's native size (e.g., 1080×1080). For full-bleed A4 print, start with images at least 2500–3500 px on the long edge so they remain crisp.
- **Compression**: JPG is fine for photos; PNG is better for graphics with flat color or transparency. SVG stays razor-sharp at any size for icons and logos.
- **Color & tone**: If your brand is muted and warm, choose images with that mood. Consistency over time builds recognition—even with different subjects.

Real Scenario — The "Looks Fine on Desktop" Trap

A café owner loved a hero shot on her laptop. On mobile, it turned to mush—too dark, subject too small. We swapped it for a close, well-lit crop of a cappuccino pouring, with steam visible. Same theme, different framing; suddenly the headline popped and the photo looked premium on a phone.

Pro Tip — Upload in Sets

Don't upload one image at a time forever. Create small, themed sets: Team portraits, Behind-the-scenes, Product close-ups, Textures. Batch uploads help you design faster because the "next best" option is already waiting in the tray.

Mini Exercise — Dual Source Test

Upload a photo from your device and search Canva's library for a similar theme (e.g., "handmade ceramics studio"). Place both on a page. Which feels more you? Write down two reasons—lighting, authenticity, color tone. Keep that note as your sourcing rule.

Cropping & Framing: Directing the Eye to the Story

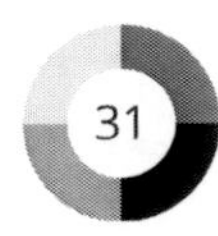

Why this matters.

Most images carry more than you need: extra background, competing subjects, empty space. Cropping creates focus; framing adds context. Together they decide what the viewer notices first and how the rest supports it.

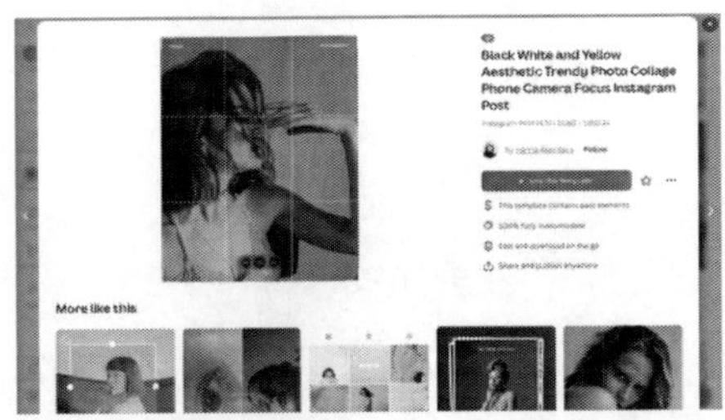

Cropping with intention.

- Select an image and click Crop.
- Instead of randomly trimming edges, ask: "Where should the eye land in one second?"
- Move the crop box until your subject sits on a strong position (rule of thirds often works: key subject on an intersection).
- For portraits, leave space in front of the face (the "look room"); for products, keep edges parallel to the frame so the object feels stable.

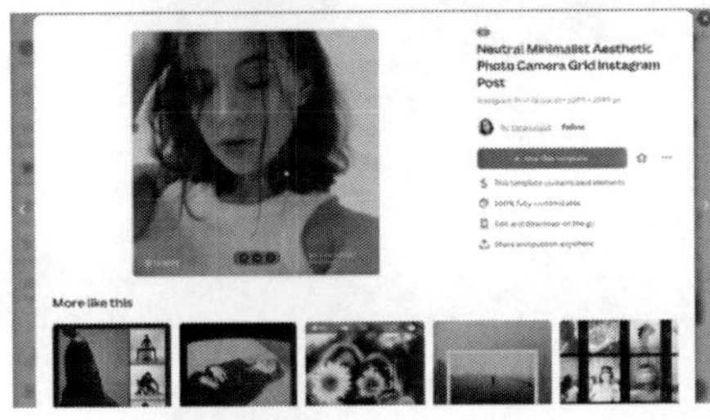

Framing to change meaning.

Frames in Canva (Elements → Frames) act like masks: drop an image into a circle to suggest "profile/identity," into a phone mockup to imply "app/tech," or into a torn paper frame for craft vibes. Frames provide instant context without adding text.

Alternative Fast Track — Use "Frames" for Carousel Consistency

When building a multi-slide carousel, pick one frame shape and use it across slides. The repeated silhouette becomes a rhythm the audience recognizes as "your series," even when photos change.

Real Scenario — From Noisy to Narrative

A travel creator used a wide cityscape on a 1080×1350 post. The skyline looked small; the caption fought for attention. We cropped tight to a single street corner with warm window light and placed the headline over a light area. Same image, but now the story was "this café at blue hour," not "a generic city."

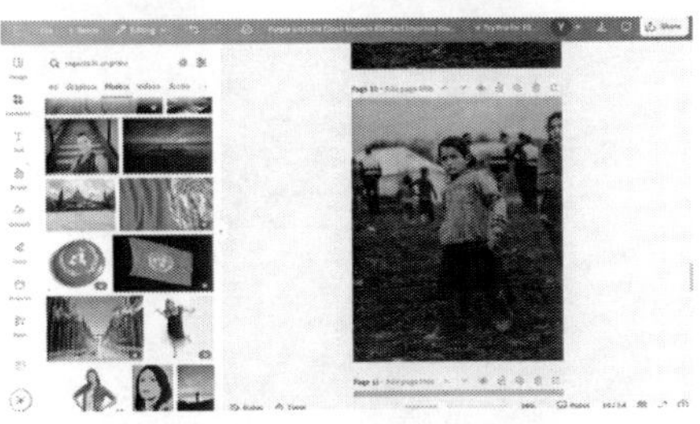

Common Pitfall — Cropping to the Edges

If you crop a face or object too close to the edge, tension spikes and the design feels cramped. Leave breathing room—especially above headlines and around key details. Negative space is not wasted space; it's the frame that makes the subject readable.

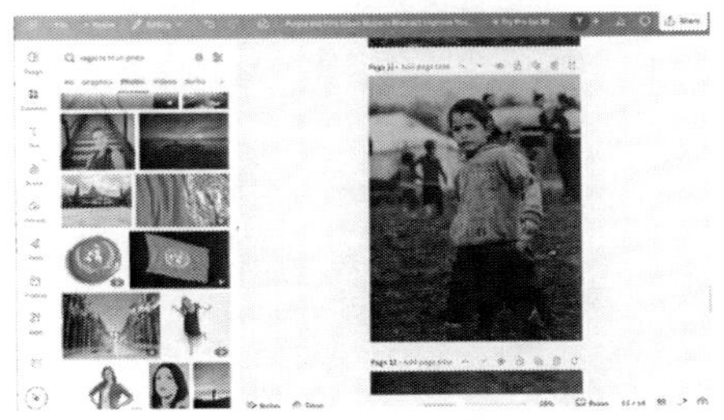

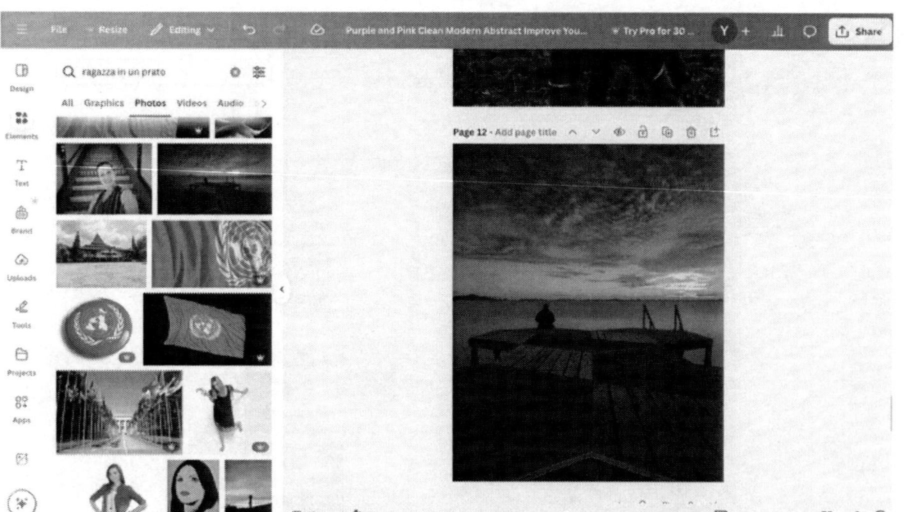

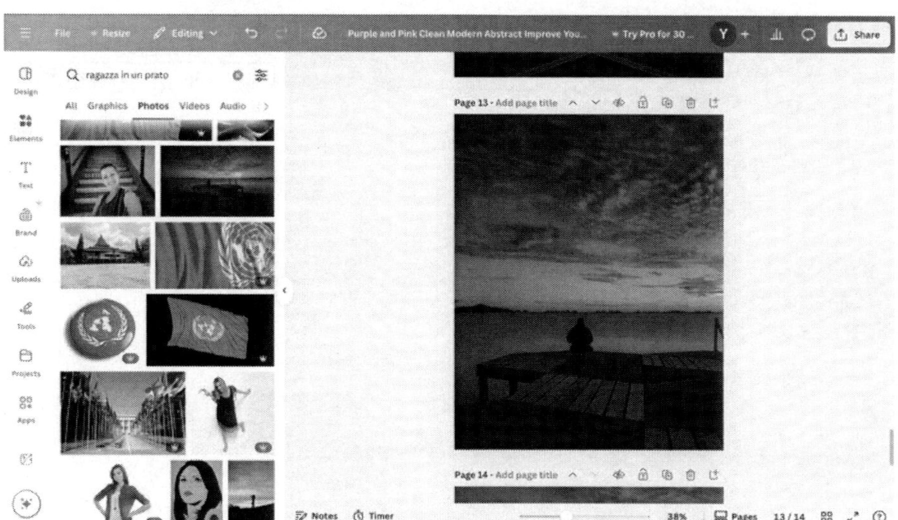

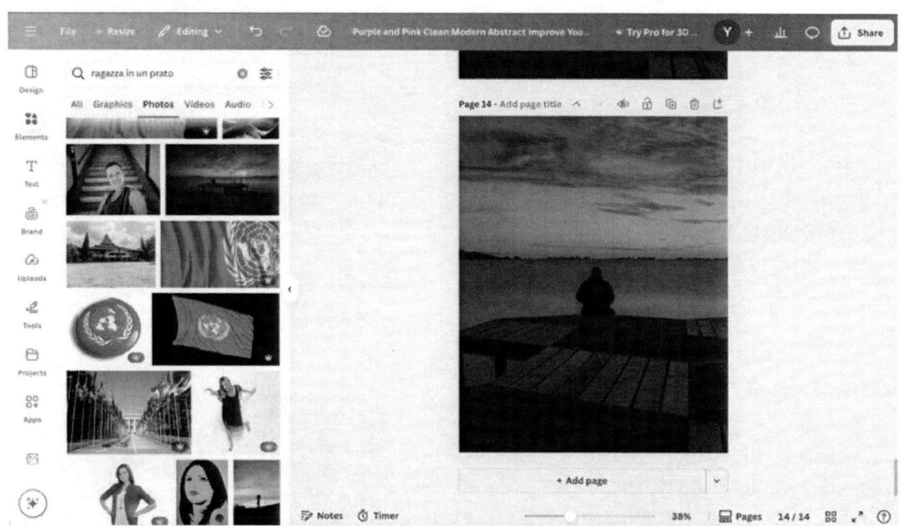

Mini Exercise — Three Crops, Three Stories

Pick one photo and create three crops:

1. Wide (environmental, subject small),
2. Medium (subject clear, some context),
3. Tight (detail shot).

Place all three on one page with the same headline.

Which tells the story best for social?

Which would you put in a brochure?

Write a one-sentence rule for when you'll choose each crop in the future.

Transparency: Balancing Photo Energy with Text Clarity

Why this matters.

Photos carry texture, contrast, and movement—great for emotion, tricky for text. Transparency lets you mediate between an energetic background and a legible message. Instead of lowering the image's brightness (which can make it dull), add a semi-transparent layer between image and text to preserve life and readability.

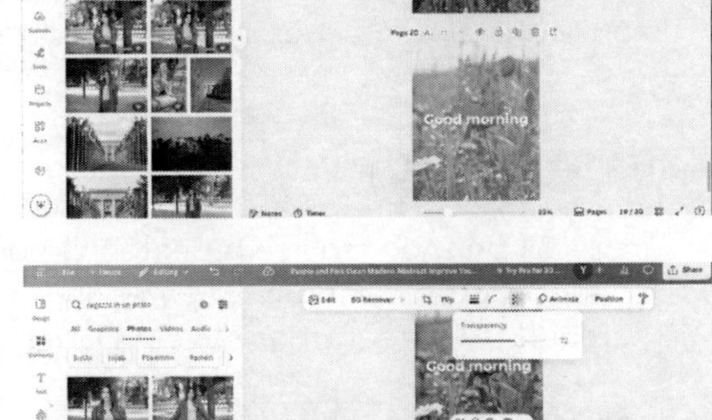

The practical recipe.

- Place a rectangle above the photo and below the headline.
- Open the transparency slider and test 30%–70% depending on background strength. Dark overlays work for light text; light overlays (or a subtle gradient) work for dark text. If your brand uses a key color, try that color at low opacity for a subtle, on-brand tint.

Beyond rectangles—shapes and gradients.

Hard rectangles are clean, but sometimes a soft gradient feels more natural, especially over complex backgrounds. A top-to-transparent gradient behind a headline can protect the first two lines while leaving the rest of the photo vibrant. Circles, ribbons, or angled shapes can also guide the eye—just use them sparingly so they support rather than compete.

Attention — Don't "Ghost" the Photo

Dropping a photo's opacity to 30% under text often kills its character. Keep the photo at 100% and adjust the layer above it. The image stays rich; the text gets its stage.

Real Scenario — YouTube Thumbnail Rescue

A tech creator had thumbnails with neon images and white text. On small screens, letters vibrated against bright details. We added a 60% dark gradient behind the title area, left the rest of the image untouched, and widened letter spacing slightly. CTR climbed—not because of clickbait, but because clarity won.

Pro Tip — Brand-Tinted Overlays

Pick your brand's darkest color and save a 40–60% overlay rectangle as a reusable component. You'll instantly harmonize mixed photo sources while reinforcing your brand palette.

Mini Exercise — The Readability Ladder

Take one busy photo and try three solutions:

1. Dark rectangle at 50% with white text,
2. Light rectangle at 50% with black text,
3. Vertical gradient (dark to transparent) at 60% under the headline.
4. Export small (1080 px) and preview on your phone. Which reads fastest? That's your default pattern.

Elements: Icons, Shapes, Lines, and the Quiet Design Grammar

Why this matters.

Elements are punctuation. They separate ideas, point attention, and create rhythm. In Canva, "Elements" includes icons, shapes, lines, stickers, and frames. These aren't decoration; they're tools for hierarchy and flow.

Icons that actually help.

Use icons when they replace repeated words or clarify categories: a phone icon before a number, a map pin for a location, a calendar for dates. Keep icon style consistent—outline with outline, solid with solid. Mismatched styles feel amateur even if the content is correct.

Shapes as structure.

Rectangles, circles, and lines build containers for text, create columns, or form call-outs. A thin line under a heading adds emphasis without shouting. Rounded rectangles can hold short CTAs; full-width bars can divide sections gracefully.

Line weight & spacing.

Elements have weight just like fonts. A 1-px hairline under a bold headline often looks elegant; a 6-px bar might overpower. Match the weight of shapes to the typographic voice—light UI = light lines, bold poster = bold shapes.

Common Pitfall — Sticker Overload

Animated stickers and playful shapes can add charm in stories or casual posts. But too many moving parts drown the message. If everything moves, nothing moves the viewer.

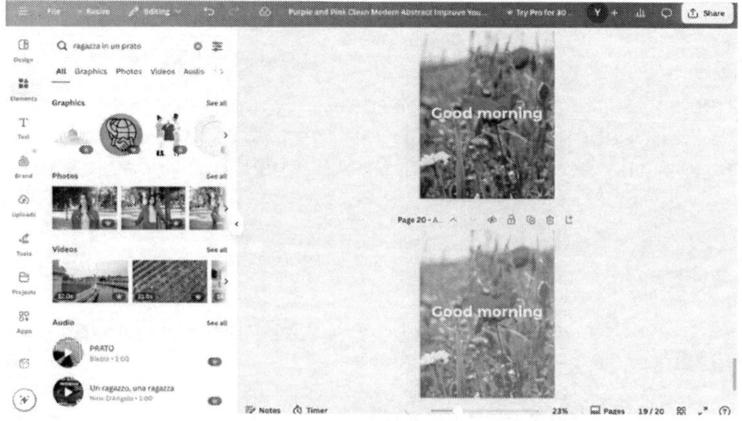

Real Scenario — A Clean Pricing Card

A founder used different icon sets for features—some rounded, some sharp. We replaced them with one consistent outline set, aligned the labels, and used a thin rule between tiers. The price card suddenly looked like the product was reliable.

Mini Exercise — Icon Consistency Audit

- Search "icons" in Elements and star a single consistent set (outline or filled).
- Build a tiny key (phone, email, map, clock). Save it to a folder named Brand → Icons. Use only those for one week.
- Notice how your designs start to feel unified.

Libraries & Asset Management: Designing Tomorrow's Speed Today

Why this matters.

A design habit without a library is a treadmill—you work hard, but don't move faster. Asset management turns creativity into a system: the images you trust, the icons that match, the overlays you reuse. When your future self logs in, the best choices are already within one click.

Folders and naming.

At minimum, create folders for Photos, Icons & Shapes, Textures/Overlays, and Brand (Logo, Palette, Fonts). Within Photos, consider subfolders by purpose (e.g., People, Product, Behind the Scenes). In Canva, you can Star assets and sort by "Starred" to quickly assemble a kit for a project.

Brand Kit (when available).

If you have Brand Kit access, load your logo, palette, and fonts. Even on free plans without full Brand Kit features, you can keep a Brand Board page—a single design with your colors, type choices, and key elements parked on it, ready to copy into any project.

Reusable components.

Save your favorite overlays, CTA buttons, dividers, and icon rows as master components on a "Components" page. When you start a new design, copy from that page instead of rebuilding. Micro-systems are how you scale.

Attention — Licensing & Mix-and-Match

If you combine Canva stock with your own photos, keep a quick note (in a text box off-canvas or a separate doc) about which assets are stock vs original. It helps maintain clarity for commercial use and handoffs to clients.

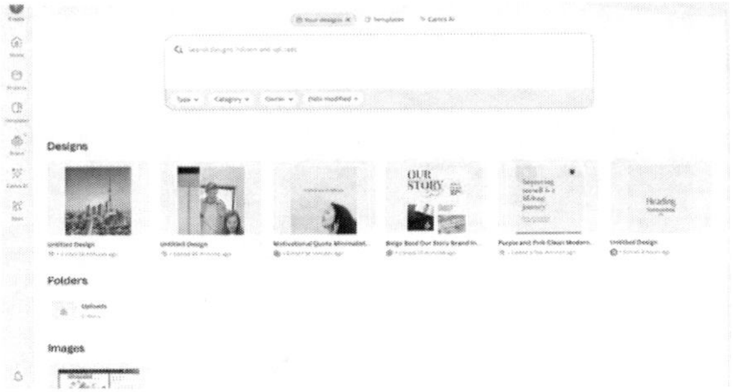

Real Scenario — The 2-Hour Weekly Batch

A creator used to spend entire evenings hunting for "the right photo." We built a library: 40 on-brand photos, a fixed icon set, and 3 overlay styles. She now batches a month of posts in two hours because the searching is over—most decisions are pre-made.

Pro Tip — Archive Aggressively

If an image never gets used, it clutters decisions. Once a month, spend ten minutes archiving or deleting unused assets. Space equals speed.

Mini Exercise — Your First System

Create a folder named Brand — Visual Library. Inside, add subfolders: Photos (People/Product/BTS), Icons & Shapes, Overlays, Components. Move at least 12 assets into the right places right now. Star your top 6. You just built tomorrow's momentum.

Putting It Together: A Small, Real Project (with reasoning)

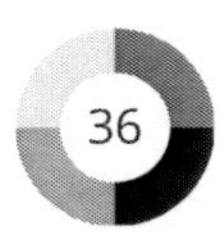

Why this matters.

Knowledge sticks when it ships. You'll create one Instagram post that uses every idea above: honest sourcing, focused cropping, supportive elements, readable text, and clean asset management.

Step-by-step, with why.

1. **Start**: Open an IG Post 1080×1080. Choose a working title like "3 Morning Habits." Naming a purpose narrows style choices.
2. **Image sourcing:** Upload a genuine photo (your desk at sunrise) or pick one Calm, warm stock shot. You'll match your brand tone.
3. **Crop for story**: Tighten to the coffee mug + notebook, placing the mug on a thirds intersection so the eye lands there first.
4. **Overlay**: Add a dark brand-tinted rectangle at ~50% behind the headline area—readability without killing mood.
5. **Type**: Place a short headline (2 lines), then a smaller subhead. Keep line lengths short for mobile.
6. **Elements**: Add a thin line under the headline to anchor it; place a small icon (sun/clock) beside the subhead if it adds clarity.
7. **Balance & spacing**: Nudge elements until spacing is even. If the photo tugs the eye away, reduce its contrast slightly with Adjust.
8. **Library**: Save the overlay and line as components to your Components page. Star the photo if it suits your style.
9. **Export**: PNG for social. Preview on phone. If text vibrates, increase overlay opacity or tighten line spacing.

You've just transformed a generic picture into a clear, branded message—fast, and with choices you can repeat.

Checklist — Images & Elements, Locked In

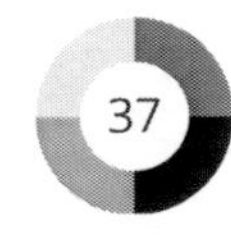

A recap consolidates progress and keeps future chapters lighter to digest. If you can say "yes" to these, you're ready to move on.

- You can source images from Uploads and Stock, choosing based on tone and quality.
- You crop with purpose, using frames when they add context rather than clutter.
- You use transparency to balance energy and legibility instead of dulling photos.
- Your elements (icons, shapes, lines) match in style and weight and serve hierarchy.
- Your library has folders, starred assets, and a components page you can reuse.

Common Mistakes — Not Errors, Just Detours (and how to correct them)

- **Mismatched Image Tone**. One cool, bluish stock photo next to a warm, golden original screams inconsistency. Solve it by grading slightly toward your brand's temperature or choosing sets with similar lighting.
- **Over-cropping the Subject**. Faces and products need breathing room. If the layout feels tense, step back one notch and let negative space frame the hero.
- **Opacity Overkill.** If everything sits under a 70% black sheet, your feed will look lifeless. Use overlays precisely where text needs protection, and keep the rest vivid.
- **Icon Soup.** Mixing outline, filled, and hand-drawn icons on one page creates visual static. Pick one family and commit.
- **Folder Chaos.** "Uploads (3,284)" is a creativity tax. Ten minutes of sorting per week returns hours of focus later.

"Do It Now" Homework — 25 Focused Minutes

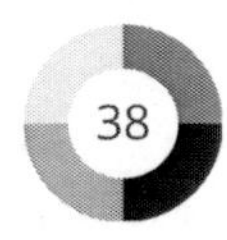

1. **Sourcing Rule (5 min).** Write your two sourcing rules (e.g., "Use my own photos for behind-the-scenes; stock only for conceptual backgrounds"). Pin them to your notebook or Brand Board page.
2. **3-Crop Study (8 min)**. Take one photo and make three crops: wide, medium, tight. Place the same headline over each. Decide which version you'll use for a carousel cover vs an inner slide.
3. **Overlay Kit (6 min).** Create three overlay components: dark brand color 50%, light brand color 40%, top-to-transparent gradient 60%. Save to Components and Star them.
4. **Library Sweep (6 min).** Build the Brand — Visual Library with subfolders and move 12 assets in. Star your top 6. You've started your system.

QR Bonus (module hub): Icon Starter Set (consistent style) + Overlay Components (3 styles) + Crop & Framing Guide (1-page). Duplicate from the QR and paste into your Brand Board.

Closing Thought

Great images don't rescue weak design—but they do supercharge strong structure. After this chapter, you can bring your world into Canva with confidence, frame it for attention, protect your message with subtle transparency, and store your assets in a system that gets faster every week. In the next chapter, we'll return to structure one last time—Export Without Errors—so that everything you've built leaves Canva looking as sharp as it does on your canvas.

Chapter 5

Exporting Confidently: Quality, Formats & Final Polish

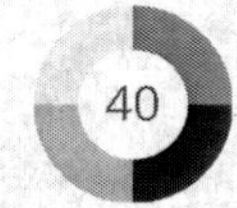

Chapter 5

Exporting Confidently: Quality, Formats & Final Polish

Export is where designs stop being ideas and start being files that travel—into phones, inboxes, printers, feeds, storefronts. You can nail color, type, images, and layout, yet lose everything in a fuzzy JPG, a bloated PDF, or a logo boxed in white. **The last mile isn't glamorous, but it's decisive:** choose the right format, set sensible quality, match dimensions to destination, and use transparency when flexibility matters. Do this well and your work looks intentional everywhere; do it poorly and even brilliant concepts arrive tired.

In this chapter, we'll make **export choices visible and repeatable.** You'll learn when PNG outperforms JPG, when PDF Standard beats PNG slides, why "max quality" isn't always quality, what "bleed" is and when to enable it, and how one checkbox ("Transparent background") turns a good asset into a versatile one. By the end, you'll export with confidence—and your designs will finally look as sharp out there as they do inside Canva.

What You'll Do in 10 Minutes (and why it matters)

A quick experiment builds intuition you can trust. In this sprint you will:

- Export the same tile as PNG (with and without transparency), JPG at medium compression, PDF Standard, and—if print-bound—PDF Print with crop marks and bleed.
- Then open each file, zoom to 200%, and compare edges, type clarity, and file weight.
- In one pass, you'll see the trade-offs most beginners guess at, and you'll start forming your personal export defaults.

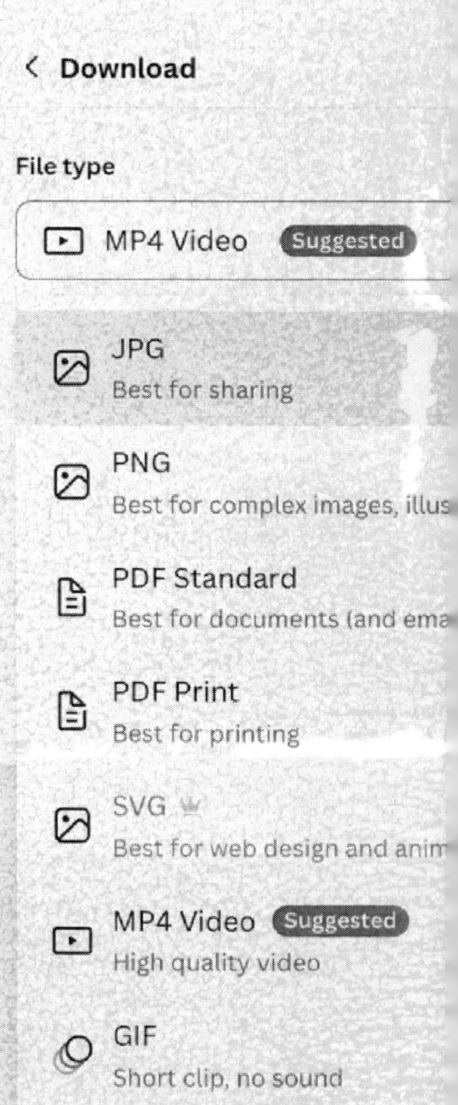

Formats: PNG, JPG, PDF — Use the Right Container

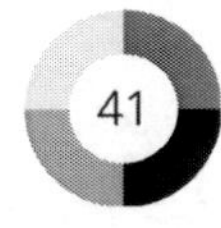

Why this matters.

Formats are containers with rules. PNG preserves crisp edges and can be transparent. JPG is compact and photographic but can't hold transparency. PDF locks layout and keeps text/vector sharp across pages and devices. When you pair message and medium correctly, you protect fidelity and reduce friction for everyone who opens your file.

PNG — crisp edges, optional transparency.

Logos, badges, stickers, UI elements, and graphics with flat color or type often look best as PNG. If the asset must float over photos or colored backgrounds, export PNG with Transparent background to remove the white box once and for all.

JPG — light weight for photos and gradients.

Photo-led posts, thumbnails, and blog images usually shine as JPG. The format compresses smoothly, keeping file sizes small and upload-friendly. Just remember: no transparency—a JPG logo will always carry a rectangle.

PDF — layout locked, vector intact.

Multi-page documents, presentations, brochures, and handouts belong in PDF. PDF Standard is perfect for screens and email; PDF Print adds crop marks and bleed for professional trimming at the printer.

Real Scenario — The Boxed Logo

A boutique exported its logo as JPG and placed it on a dark hero image. The white rectangle looked amateurish. Re-exporting as PNG with transparency solved it instantly—same design, professional result.

Pro Tip — Thumbnail vs Handout

If you're sending slides to be read on-screen, export PDF Standard (text stays vector-sharp, file stays light). If you're posting just the cover slide to social, export that single page as JPG for speed and platform-friendly compression.

Mini Exercise — Two Exports, One Truth

- Create a simple wordmark inside a rounded shape.
- Export as JPG and PNG (transparent).
- Place both over a photo background.

The difference you see is the rule you'll follow forever.

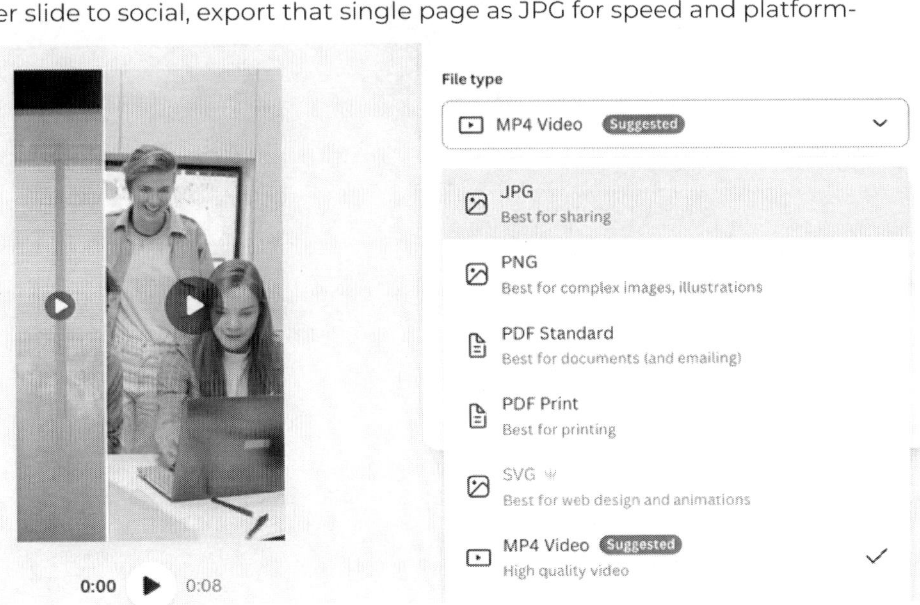

Quality: Sharp Enough, Small Enough

Why this matters.

"Max quality" isn't a strategy. Platforms compress uploads, clients dislike huge attachments, and printers need the right data—not the heaviest file. Quality is a dial you set per destination.

Social: photo-led posts.

For Instagram, LinkedIn, and Twitter/X, JPG around 80% often looks indistinguishable from lossless while cutting size dramatically. If your tile is mostly flat graphics or type, PNG may keep edges crisper—check both at 200% zoom.

Documents: screen reading.

Export decks and brochures as PDF Standard so body text stays vector-clean and images compress sensibly. Recipients can search, copy text, and print desktop-friendly handouts without ballooning file sizes.

Print: production-ready.

Use PDF Print, enable Bleed and Crop marks when a design runs to the edge. The printer will trim precisely to the final size; the bleed prevents unexpected white rims.

Real Scenario — The 10 MB Carousel

A creator exported a 10-slide carousel as max-quality PNGs; uploads stalled and IG recompressed anyway. Switching to JPG ~80% reduced each slide to ~1 MB with no visible loss on mobile.

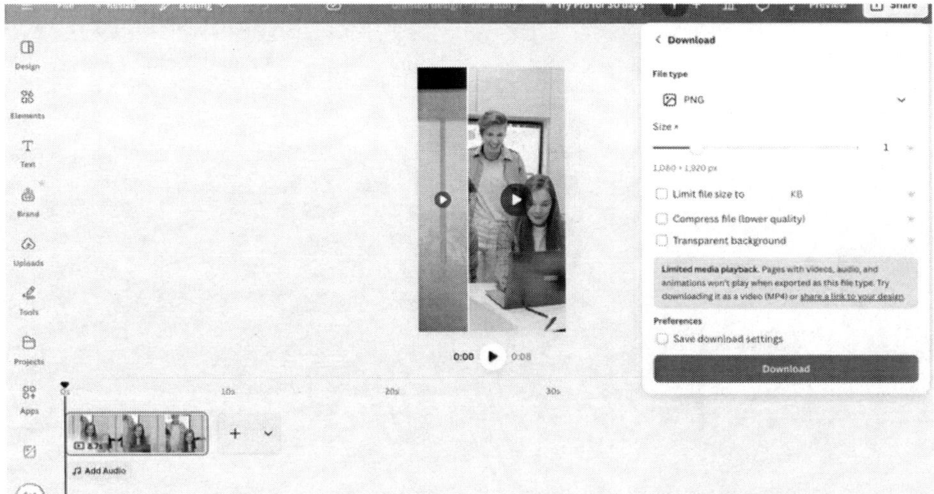

Pro Tip - The 200% QC Rule

Open your export and zoom to 200% on a headline and icon.

If edges look soft, bump quality up one notch. If they look identical across two settings, choose the smaller file.

Mini Exercise — A/B Compression

- Export the same tile as JPG 80% and PNG.
- Compare at 100%/200% on a phone and laptop.
- Record your default per asset type on your Brand Board ("Photo tiles → JPG 80%; Flat graphics → PNG.")

Dimensions: Design for the Destination

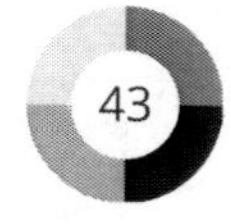

Why this matters.

Wrong dimensions force platforms to crop or scale your work, costing you clarity. Starting with the correct preset (1080×1080 Post, 1080×1920 Story, 1280×720 Thumbnail, A4/Letter) prevents cut-off headlines and awkward margins.

Start right; resize smart.

Choose the proper preset before you design. If you must adapt, use Resize to create the new canvas, then re-compose: adjust type sizes, nudge margins, reposition imagery. A good resize is a design act, not a stretch.

Safe zones and masks.

Stories need vertical flow with essential text away from top/bottom edges; thumbnails need central focus and big type; LinkedIn crops differently across placements. Designing for the real frame is the difference between "fine" and "professional."

Real Scenario — Cropped Call-to-Action

A square tile posted as a Story lost its bottom CTA to auto-cropping. Reframing in 1080×1920, lifting the CTA, and increasing top/bottom padding restored legibility and intent.

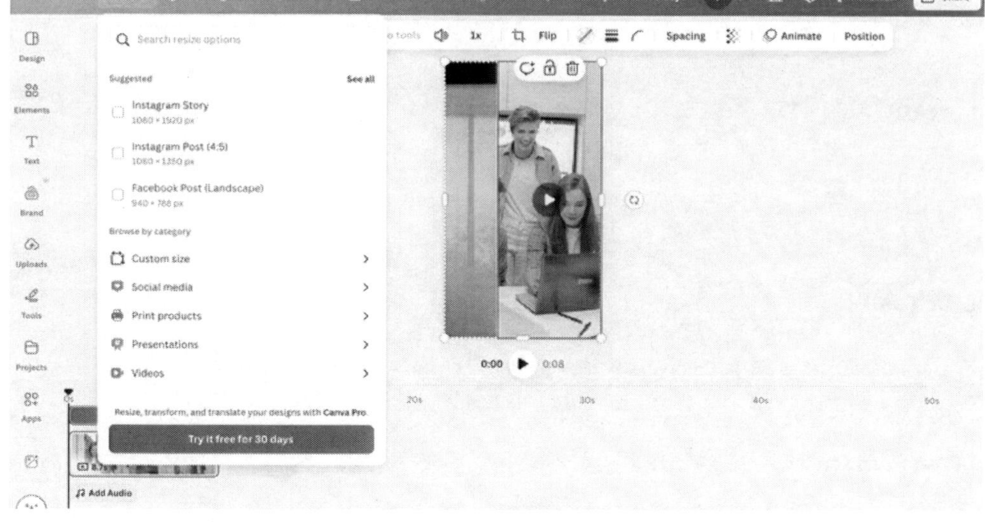

Pro Tip - Two Master Canvases

- Keep a Square Master (1080×1080) and a Story Master (1080×1920) template with guides and default type scales.
- Duplicating from masters saves time and preserves rhythm across formats.

Mini Exercise — Twin Composition Test

- Design one cover tile, then adapt it to Story.
- On your phone, compare where the eye lands first and how quickly the headline reads.
- Write a one-line rule you'll apply next time (e.g., "Story = larger lead line + higher CTA.")

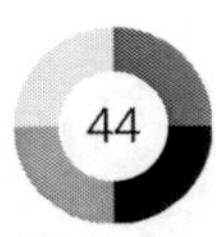

Transparency: Make Assets That Work Everywhere

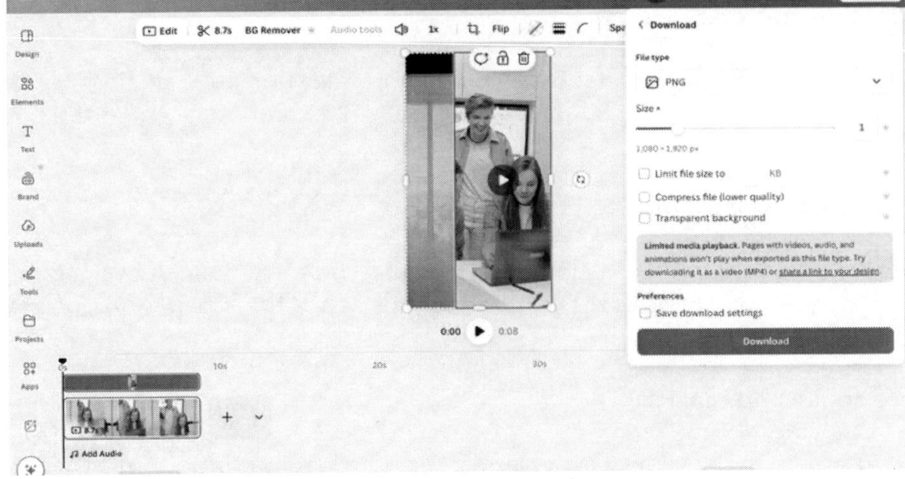

Why this matters.

When logos, badges, and sticker-style graphics need to sit on photos, colors, or video frames, transparency keeps them adaptable—and keeps you out of the white-box trap.

How to export with transparency.

Choose PNG, tick Transparent background, then export. You'll get only the marks—not the canvas. This is essential for overlays, mockups, and video lower-thirds.

Watch for halos.

If you designed on white, a faint fringe can appear over dark photos due to anti-aliasing. Test on white, black, and photo backgrounds. If halos show, tighten artwork edges or export placed on a neutral mid-gray background first.

Real Scenario — Apparel Mockup Fail → Fix

A merch designer placed a JPG logo on a t-shirt photo—instant white square. Re-exported as PNG (transparent), the mark blended naturally; a light Multiply effect on the mockup made it feel printed, not pasted.

Pro Tip — Three-Background Test

After exporting a transparent asset, drop it onto a white tile, a black tile, and a busy photo. If it reads on all three, ship it.

Mini Exercise — Badge to Everywhere

Create a small badge. Export PNG (transparent). Place it on three previous posts and one video frame. If it never carries a box and remains legible, your export is production-ready.

Checklist: Export, Locked In

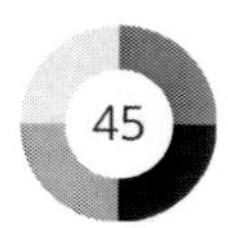

You can now:

- Choose PNG / JPG / PDF deliberately,
- Dial quality to balance sharpness and size,
- Match dimensions to the destination (and re-compose when resizing),
- Export transparency for assets that must float over anything.

If you can explain why for each choice, you're no longer guessing—you're finishing like a pro.

Common Mistakes — And Gentle Fixes

- JPG Logos with White Boxes. Re-export as PNG (transparent) and update your Brand Board note so it never happens again.
- Overkill File Sizes. Social doesn't need lossless. Use JPG ~80% for photo-heavy tiles; reserve PNG for flat graphics and type.
- Wrong Canvas, Wrong Crop. Start with the right preset. If adapting, Resize → Re-compose (don't just stretch).
- No Bleed for Print. White rims are preventable. Export PDF Print with Bleed + Crop marks and confirm specs with your printer.

"Do It Now" Homework — 20 Focused Minutes

Defaults (6 min)
On your Brand Board, add a tiny table:
IG Post → JPG 80% | IG Story → PNG (type over photo) or JPG 80% (photo-only) | Print flyer → PDF Print (bleed).

Two-Zoom QC (4 min)

Export a finished tile. Inspect at 100%/200%. If edges blur, bump quality; if identical but heavy, step down.

Transparent Toolkit (5 min)

Export your logo, badge, and CTA button as PNG (transparent). Test on white, black, photo.

Dimension Sanity Check (5 min)

Duplicate a square tile to Story via Resize. Re-compose type and margins. Preview on your phone before shipping.

Closing Thought

Finishing well is a creative act. When you pair the right format with the right quality, choose honest dimensions, and use transparency with intent, your work arrives in the world exactly as you imagined it—crisp, confident, and trustworthy. Export is not an afterthought; it's the seal on your craft.

Module 2 Canva for Social Media

From Random Posts to a Consistent Voice

Module 2 – Canva for Social Media

From Random Posts to a Consistent Voice

Social media is where most brands live—or die. A website is static, a brochure is handed out once, but your **Instagram, LinkedIn, TikTok, or Facebook** feed is alive every single day. And yet, for most beginners, social media design is pure chaos: random colors, inconsistent fonts, posts that feel disconnected from each other. The result? Even good ideas look unprofessional, and followers scroll past without remembering who you are.

But here's the good news: consistency is not magic. It's a system. And Canva makes that system accessible to anyone—even if you've never studied design. With the right templates, palettes, and batching habits, you can produce a month of content in just a few focused hours. More importantly, your feed starts to look like a brand rather than a string of one-offs.

Think about what happens when your posts align: your colors repeat, your typography speaks with one tone, your logos sit in the same corner, your photos share a mood. Suddenly, people recognize your work at a glance. That recognition is trust. And trust is what social media, beneath all the noise, is really about.

This module will take you from sporadic posting to a **scalable content system.** You won't just design pretty posts; you'll learn how to batch 30 posts at a time, adapt them for multiple platforms, and keep everything on-brand without reinventing the wheel. Along the way, you'll create a Content Pack you can duplicate and adapt forever—your personal social media design engine.

What You'll Do in 10 Minutes (and why it matters)

To warm up, we'll start with a micro-sprint:

- Duplicate a social media post template.
- Swap in your logo and palette.
- Write three different headlines.
- Export the posts and preview them on your phone.

In just 10 minutes, you'll see how fast "one post" can become "a set." That shift—from single to system—is what unlocks scale.

What This Module Covers

By the end of Module 2, you will:

- Master Canva templates for social posts (static, carousel, story, reel cover).
- Batch-create 30 posts in a session, using duplication and small variations.
- Adapt posts across platforms, keeping brand voice consistent while respecting each format.
- Build a content calendar with your designs, so posting feels planned, not frantic.
- Export correctly for each platform, so posts look sharp everywhere.

Target Audience

This module is for beginners, solopreneurs, side hustlers, and students who want to look professional on social without hiring a designer. It's also for small businesses tired of inconsistent feeds and ready to build a visual system that scales.

Measurable Outcomes

By the end of Module 2, you will be able to:

- Design and export 30 coordinated social media posts in Canva.
- Apply your brand logo, palette, and fonts consistently across posts.
- Adapt a single design into at least three different formats (Post, Story, Carousel).
- Create a starter content calendar populated with your Canva designs.

Chapter 1

Social Formats Made Easy: Posts, Ratios & Platform Consistency

Chapter 1

Social Formats Made Easy: Posts, Ratios & Platform Consistency

Imagine meeting someone who wears a different outfit every time you see them—so different you're not even sure it's the same person. That's how your audience feels when your posts look inconsistent across platforms. Instagram loves squares, TikTok thrives on tall verticals, YouTube runs on thumbnails, and LinkedIn expects polished professionalism. If you take one design and force it everywhere, you break recognition.

Consistency is not sameness—it's coherence. It means your colors, fonts, logo, and tone stay recognizable, while the format adapts to the frame. Canva's templates make this easy, but only if you understand each platform's native language.

In this chapter, we'll walk through the four **major social ecosystems—Instagram, TikTok, YouTube, and LinkedIn**—and break down their formats one by one. You'll learn how to design posts, stories, thumbnails, banners, and carousels that adapt without losing identity. By the end, you'll know how to translate one idea across multiple platforms so it feels like you everywhere, not a patchwork of random content.

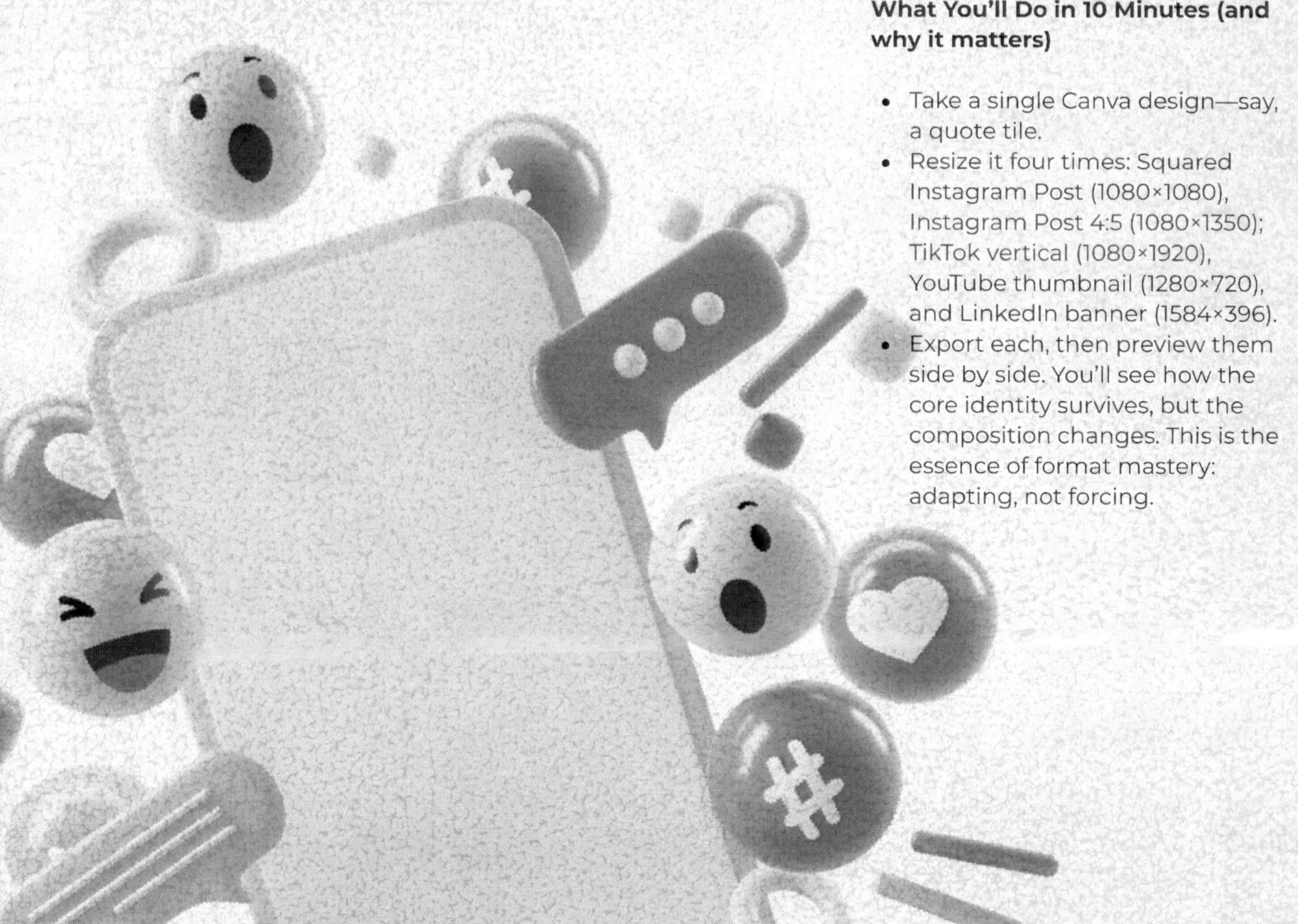

What You'll Do in 10 Minutes (and why it matters)

- Take a single Canva design—say, a quote tile.
- Resize it four times: Squared Instagram Post (1080×1080), Instagram Post 4:5 (1080×1350); TikTok vertical (1080×1920), YouTube thumbnail (1280×720), and LinkedIn banner (1584×396).
- Export each, then preview them side by side. You'll see how the core identity survives, but the composition changes. This is the essence of format mastery: adapting, not forcing.

Instagram: The Post, the Story, the Carousel

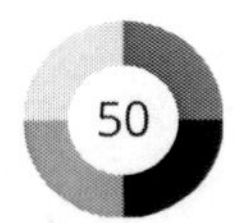

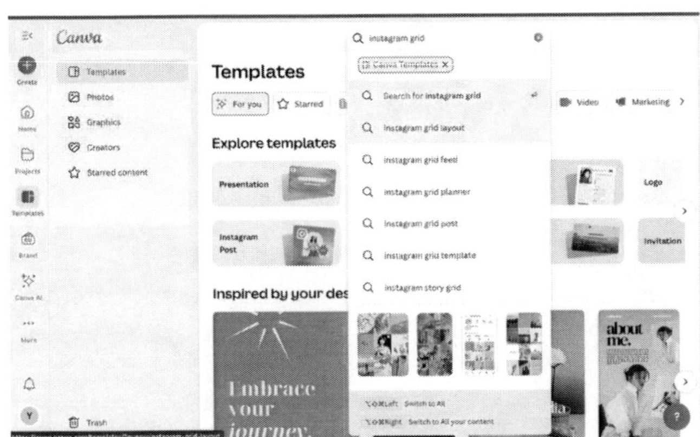

Why this matters.

Instagram is still the cornerstone for many creators and small businesses. The platform supports multiple formats, each with different rules: grid posts, carousels, stories, reels covers, highlights. Mastering all of them ensures your brand feels native, not recycled.

Core formats:

- **Grid post**: Instagram Post 4:5 (1080×1350) — new timeless, clean, consistent in profile view.
- **Carousel:** multiple 1080×1350 posts swiped in sequence, perfect for storytelling.
- **Stories/Reels:** 1080×1920 vertical, occupying the full screen.
- **Reel cover**: still 1080×1920 but must be designed with safe zones so the cover looks good in the square grid preview.
- **Highlights**: story icons, usually round, small (200×200 recommended).

Real Scenario — The Personal Trainer

A creator posted random sizes: sometimes 4:5, sometimes landscape. His feed looked chaotic. Once he locked everything to 1080×1350 and designed matching stories, his grid started to look like a polished portfolio.

Pro Tip — Safe Zone for Reels Covers

Always place text and logos in the center square of your reel cover. That way, when Instagram crops it for the grid, nothing gets cut.

Mini Exercise — Carousel Consistency

Create a 3-slide carousel with one headline repeated across all slides. Export and swipe on your phone. Does the flow feel smooth? Adjust margins until it reads like a story.

TikTok: Vertical First, Speed Always

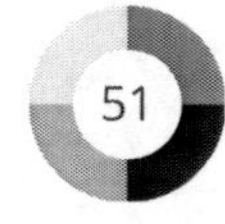

Why this matters.

TikTok is full immersion: 1080×1920 vertical video. No side margins, no half-crops. Design here must respect safe zones—bottom for captions, right for buttons. Canva lets you make animated slides or short video posts that feel native.

Core formats:

- **Vertical video**: 1080×1920 — main content.
- **Safe zones:** keep text and CTAs in upper-middle; avoid bottom third and right edge.
- **Profile picture & cover**: not designed in Canva but must harmonize.
- **Ad creatives (Spark Ads)**: same 1080×1920, but focus on strong hooks in first 3 seconds.

Real Scenario — The Language Tutor

You can repurpose Instagram slides by simply uploading them to TikTok. The text got covered by captions. After redesigning with safe zones in mind, retention rates doubled.

Attention — Platform Compression

TikTok compresses heavily. Export as MP4, 1080×1920 with medium compression; overloading quality often backfires.

Pro Tip — The "Upper Third Rule"

Always position text in the upper third. That area remains visible across most UI overlays.

Mini Exercise — Resize with Intention

Take a square quote tile. Resize to 1080×1920. Move headline to upper third, place logo top-left. Export and preview in TikTok mockup.

YouTube: Thumbnails, Banners, End Screens

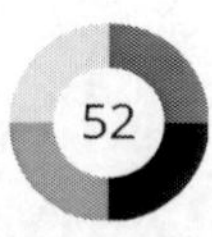

Why this matters.

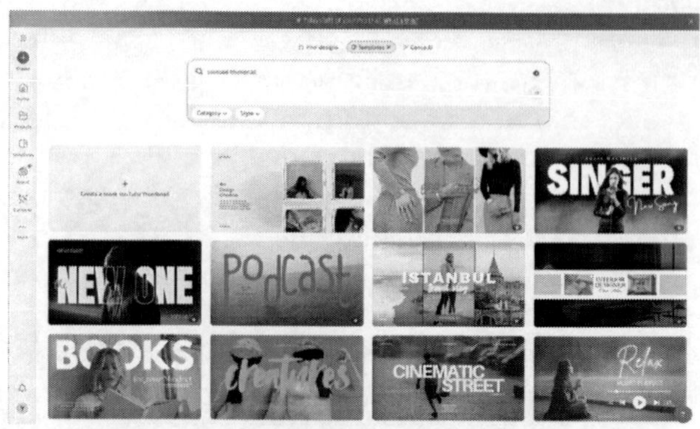

On YouTube, people click before they listen. Your thumbnail is your first handshake.

But the ecosystem also includes banners and end screens—spaces where brand consistency builds trust.

Core formats:

- **Thumbnail: 1280×720 (16:9)** — bold text, clear image, CTR driver.
- **Channel banner: 2560×1440 (safe area 1546×423)** — visible differently on TV, desktop, mobile.
- **End screen**: 1920×1080 overlay — design space for CTAs, playlists, or subscribe buttons.
- **Shorts**: 1080×1920 vertical video, but designed for scrollable feeds.

Real Scenario — Tech Reviewer

Their content was high-quality but thumbnails were dull screenshots. Once they designed custom thumbnails with bold type + brand accent, CTR rose 40%.

Pro Tip — The Blink Test

Shrink your thumbnail to 10% size. If it's still readable, it works. If not, simplify text.

Common Pitfall — Banner Safe Area

Many creators design banners too wide; text gets cut on mobile. Always check safe area guides.

Mini Exercise — Thumbnail Sprint

Design one 1280×720 thumbnail. Export and scale down to 100px. Does it still communicate?

LinkedIn: Professional Polish

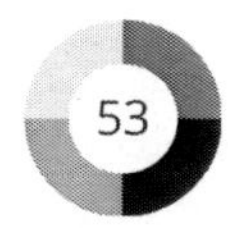

Why this matters.

LinkedIn is where business credibility is judged. Poorly formatted posts or cut-off banners suggest carelessness. With the right formats, your profile becomes a portfolio.

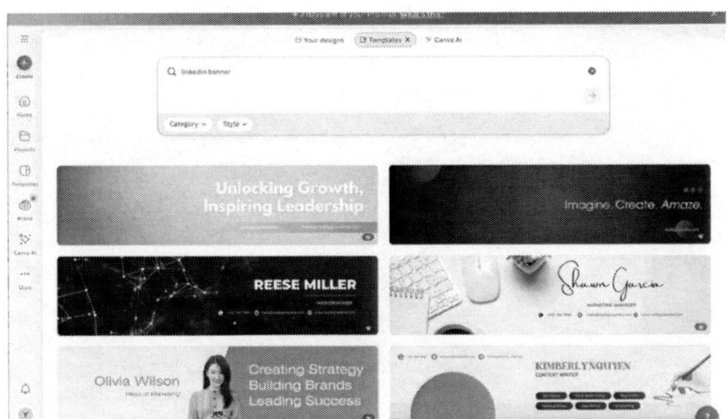

Core formats:

- **Feed post**: 1200×1200 (square) or 1200×628 (landscape).
- **Carousel posts**: uploaded as PDF multi-page (Canva export directly).
- **Company banner**: 1128×191 — narrow, needs clean type.
- **Personal banner:** 1584×396 — wide, must keep key info centered.

Real Scenario — Consultant Brand Upgrade

A consultant's banner had text pushed to the edge. On mobile, it cut off her website. Re-centered in Canva, the new banner read clearly across devices, improving credibility.

Attention — Text Hierarchy

LinkedIn users skim. Keep banners clean: logo, tagline, maybe one CTA. Posts should focus on clarity over decoration.

Pro Tip — PDF Carousels Win

Instead of static images, export educational content as PDF carousels. LinkedIn treats them like slide decks—perfect for storytelling.

Mini Exercise — Personal Banner Fix

Design a 1584×396 banner. Place text only in center safe zone. Export, preview on desktop and mobile. Adjust until consistent.

Checklist — Formats & Consistency

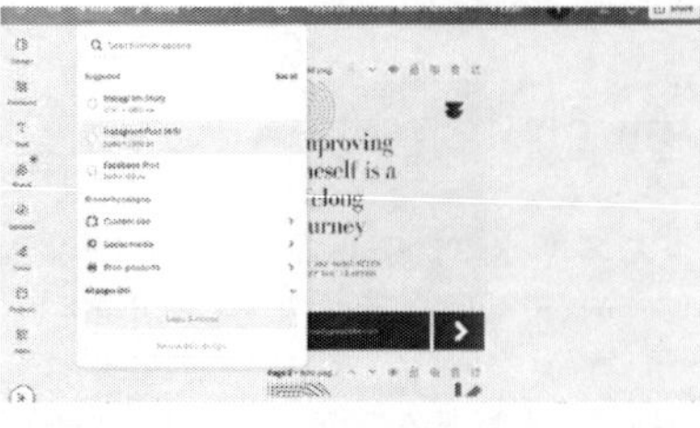

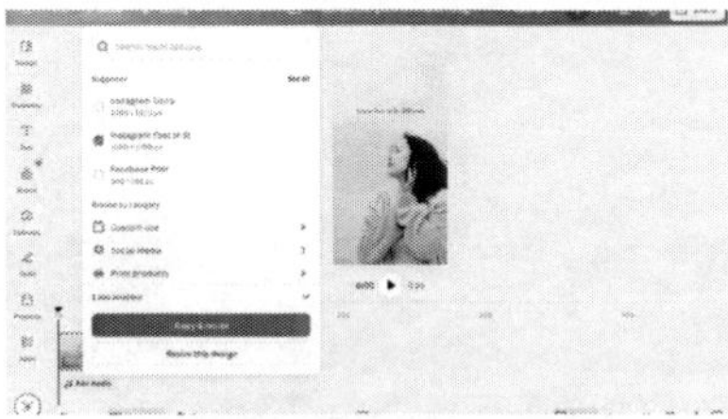

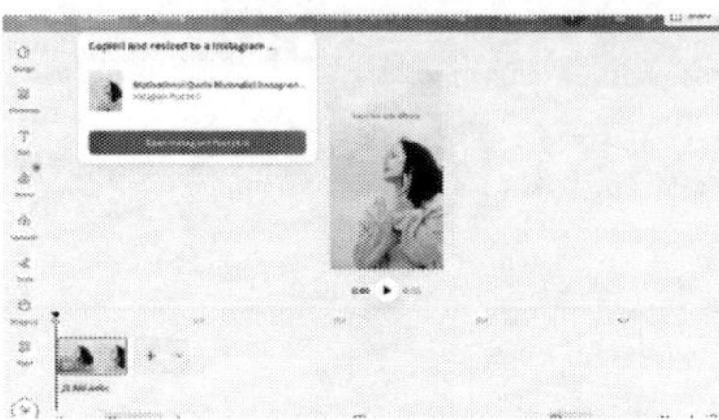

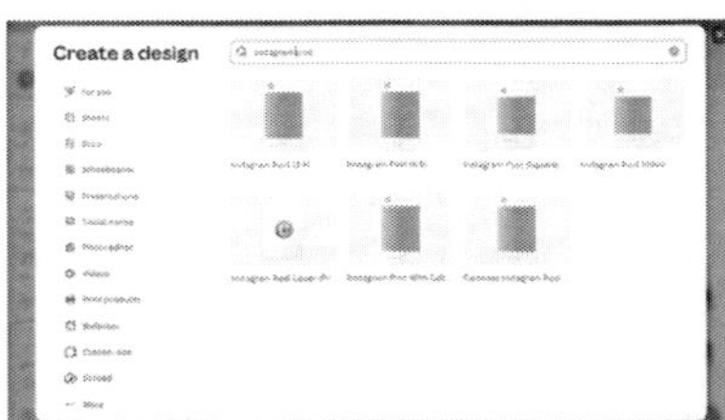

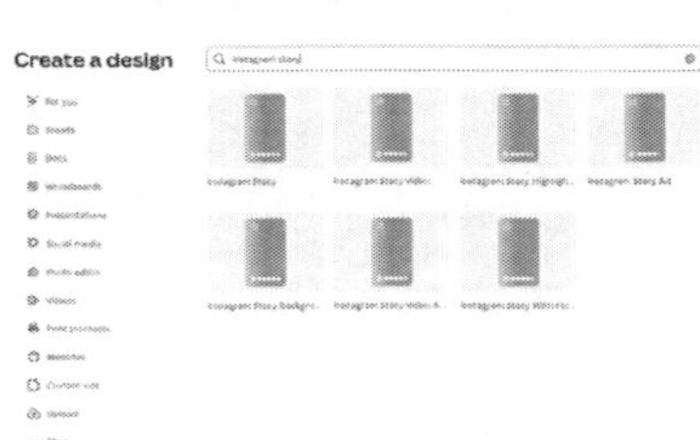

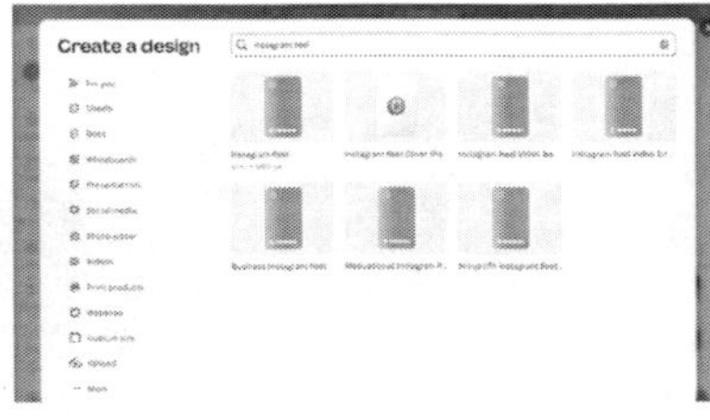

Checklist — Formats & Consistency

- Instagram posts, carousels, stories, reels covers designed natively.
- TikTok verticals with safe zones respected.
- YouTube thumbnails, banners, end screens sized correctly.
- LinkedIn posts, carousels, banners adapted to safe areas.
- Brand elements (logo, colors, fonts) coherent across all.

Common Mistakes — And How to Fix Them

- One-size-fits-all exports. Fix: resize with Canva's tool and re-compose.
- Ignoring safe zones. Fix: test with overlays before publishing.
- Overloading text. Fix: simplify, bold key words only.
- Banner cut-offs. Fix: always check mobile safe areas.

"Do It Now" Homework — 30 Minutes

1. Take one design (quote or CTA).
2. Resize it into Instagram (1080×1080, 1080×1920), TikTok (1080×1920), YouTube thumbnail (1280×720), LinkedIn banner (1584×396).
3. Export all.
4. Preview on each platform (mockup or actual upload).
5. Write down 3 rules for your brand ("Logo always top-right," "Text max 5 words in thumbnails," "Banners: text centered only")

.

QR Bonus (Module Hub):

- Dimension Cheat Sheet for all platforms.
- 20 Social Templates for posts + carousels.
- Thumbnail Starter Kit (5 styles) tested for CTR.

Closing Thought

Adapting formats isn't busywork—it's respect for the medium. When your posts fit every frame, your brand feels intentional and professional. Your followers won't think "nice resize"—they'll think "I know this brand, I trust them." And that recognition, across Instagram, TikTok, YouTube, and LinkedIn, is the first real step to social authority.

Chapter 2

Instagram & TikTok Creation: Stories, Reels, Carousels & Fast Hooks

Chapter 2

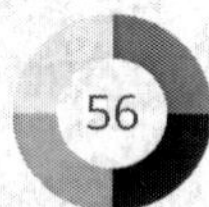

Instagram & TikTok Creation: Stories, Reels, Carousels & Fast Hooks

If you want visibility today, **you can't ignore Instagram and TikTok**. These two platforms dominate the attention economy. They're where culture spreads, where trends begin, and where brands—personal or business—earn trust or vanish. But here's the catch: they reward speed, clarity, and emotion, not clutter.

A good design for Instagram or TikTok is not about decoration. It's about function: **grabbing attention in less than three seconds, delivering value fast, and leaving a clear next step** (a hook at the start, a CTA at the end). This isn't just design—it's choreography. Every slide, story, or reel cover is a move in a sequence that keeps viewers watching and acting.

Many beginners treat Instagram posts as random pretty cute designs, or TikTok covers as afterthoughts. But real creators know: consistency of brand + platform-native storytelling = growth. If you align your palette, fonts, and logo with strong hooks and calls to action, your content becomes recognizable, trustworthy, and sharable.

In this chapter, we'll walk through the main content types on IG and TikTok:

- Posts that fit the grid but also work in feed.
- Stories that invite interaction.
- Carousels that tell a story in swipes.
- Reel covers that protect recognition and readability.
- Hooks and CTAs that make people stop scrolling and take action.

By the end, you won't just be designing "pretty posts." You'll be creating narratives people engage with—a system of visuals and words tuned for platforms that never sleep.

What You'll Do in 10 Minutes (and why it matters)

Take one idea (e.g., "3 tips to stay focused").

- Make a square post (1080×1080) with headline + subtext.
- Duplicate as a Story (1080×1920) with vertical flow.
- Build a 3-slide Carousel version (same fonts/colors).
- Add a Reel Cover with logo centered and safe zones respected.
- Preview them side by side. You'll see the power of repurposing: one idea → four native assets.

Instagram Posts: Your Visual Anchor

Why this matters.

Posts are still the foundation of Instagram. They live in the grid, get shared in feed, and become your portfolio. They must be clear, consistent, and instantly recognizable.

Best practices:

- Size: 1080×1350 (4:5).
- Headline clarity: 3–5 words max, big and bold.
- Logo placement: consistent corner (usually bottom-right).
- Palette rotation: apply your chosen colors strategically, not randomly.

Real Scenario — The Fitness Coach

A creator used random Canva templates. Her feed looked mismatched. Once she locked a color palette (navy + neon green), her grid became coherent. Clients noticed: "I know it's your post before I read it."

Pro Tip — Grid View Audit

Duplicate 9 posts and arrange in Canva's grid. Does it feel like a family? If not, adjust palette and fonts.

Mini Exercise

Design 3 posts. Use same font, logo, color accents. Export and view on your phone grid. Do they hold together?

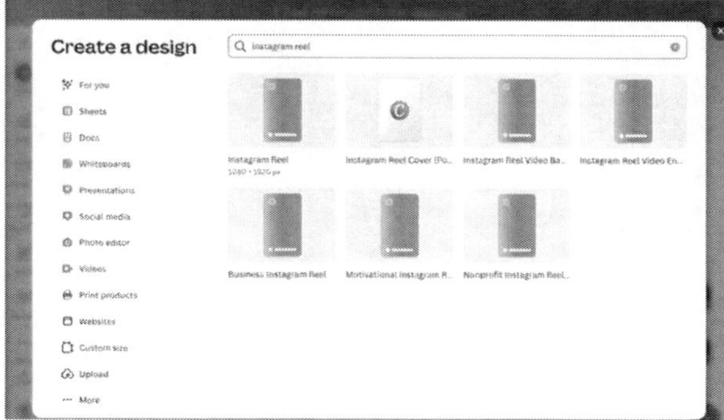

Instagram Stories: Interactive Flow

Why this matters.

Stories are full-screen, ephemeral, but powerful. They drive engagement, clicks, and personality. Design here must respect vertical flow and safe zones.

Best practices:

- Size: 1080×1920 (9:16).
- Hierarchy: one main message per story.
- Interactive elements: leave space for polls, stickers, questions.
- Visual rhythm: alternate static slides, short videos, and CTA slides.

Real Scenario — The Café Launch

A coffee shop announced a new latte via a 3-slide

- Story: Slide 1—photo of cup with headline. Slide 2—poll ("Would you try it?").
- Slide 3—CTA with swipe-up. Result: 300+ responses in one day.

Attention — Don't Overstuff

Stories are not posters. If everything screams, nothing is heard. Keep one clear idea per slide.

Mini Exercise

Turn one square post into a 3-slide Story sequence. Export and preview vertically.

Instagram Carousels: Swipe to Storytell

Why this matters.

Carousels are the secret weapon for engagement. People swipe more than they read captions. Each slide is a beat in your story.

Best practices:

- Size: 1080×1350 (4:5) for each slide.
- Slide 1: big hook.
- Slides 2–n: value bites (tips, steps, quotes).
- Final slide: CTA (follow, share, comment).

Real Scenario — Marketing Consultant

Turn blog posts into 8-slide carousels. Engagement tripled: same content, better delivery.

Pro Tip — Visual Rhythm

Alternate bold text slides with image slides. It keeps attention alive.

Mini Exercise

Build a 3-slide carousel: Hook → Tip → CTA. Export and swipe-test.

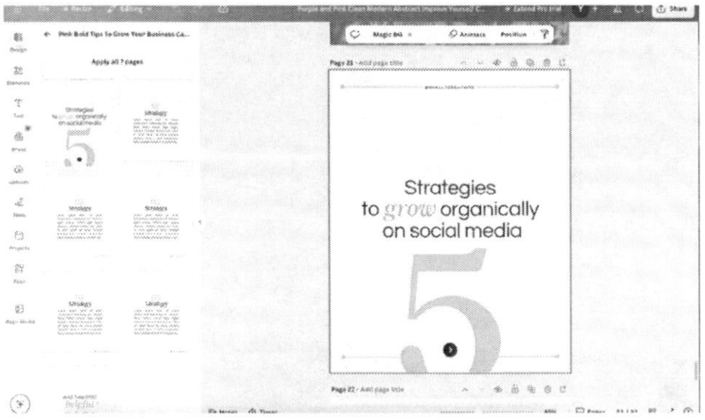

Reel Covers: Protecting Your Grid

Why this matters.

Reels are powerful, but their covers live on your profile grid. If covers aren't designed with safe zones, text gets cropped, leaving your grid messy.

Best practices:

- Size: 1080×1920, but design inside central 1080×1440 safe zone for grid view.
- Headline: short, bold, central.
- Logo: consistent corner.

Real Scenario — Lifestyle Creator

Imagine this: Anita is an influencer. She had random covers—her grid looked chaotic. Once she standardized covers with consistent fonts and palette, her profile felt professional.

Pro Tip — Use Templates

Create one Reel Cover template. Duplicate for each reel, only swap headline + image.

Mini Exercise

Design a Reel Cover with safe zone guides. Export and preview in grid mockup.

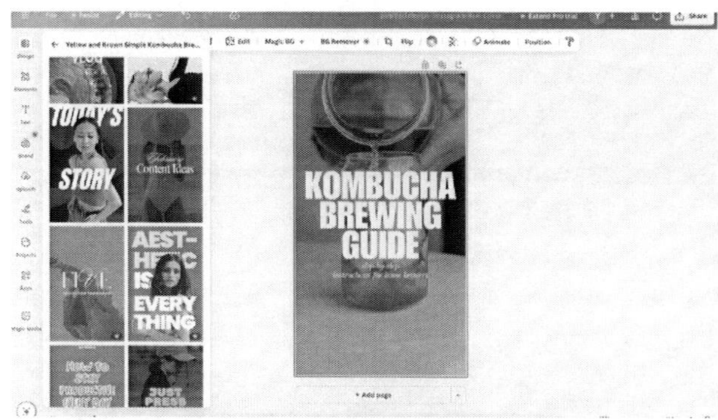

Hooks & CTAs: The Invisible Design Layer

Why this matters.

Great design fails if nobody stops to read. Hooks and CTAs are the invisible layer of design strategy: the words and placements that move people.

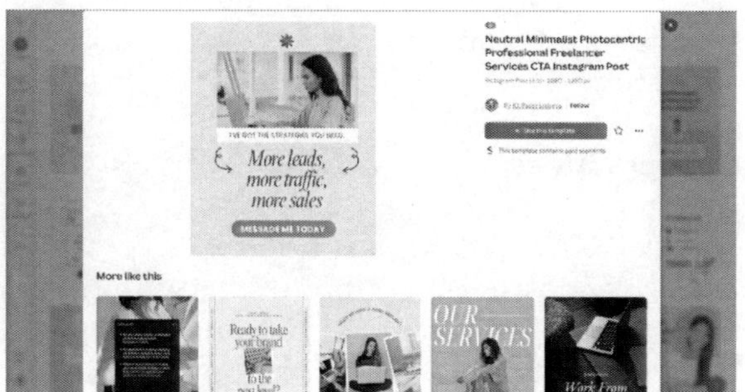

Hooks:

Hooks grab attention in seconds.
Think of them as your digital handshake:
bold, quick, and impossible to ignore. Effective hooks are:

- Short, bold, urgent. "Stop doing this..."
- Curiosity-driven. "Ever wondered why...?"
- Specific and numbered. "3 hacks you need today."

CTAs:

If hooks pull people in, CTAs tell them what to do next. Every piece of content needs a clear next step — simple, visible, and natural.

- Direct actions: "Follow for more," "Save this tip," "Click the link in bio," "Write this word and I'll send you freebies."
- Placed strategically: end of a carousel, final story frame, or caption of a reel.
- Visually emphasized: buttons, bold highlights, or standout typography.

Real Scenario — Small Biz Growth

A small bakery kept posting beautiful photos — cakes, pastries, specials — but nothing moved. People liked, scrolled, and left. Then they added one line to every carousel: "DM us to order." No redesign, no ads, no gimmicks.
Within a month, Instagram orders tripled. The visuals already worked; what was missing was direction. The CTA became the bridge between attention and action.
The design stayed the same — the strategy evolved.

Attention Rule — Don't Shout Twice

One of the biggest mistakes in design communication is trying to win attention with volume — stacking multiple hooks, arrows, and CTAs as if shouting louder would make people care more. It doesn't. It dilutes focus. Every asset should have a single moment of entry (the hook) and a single direction to exit (the CTA). The first stops the scroll. The second gives purpose to that stop. Anything in between should support those two anchors, not compete with them. If you have three messages shouting for attention, the viewer hears none. If you have one message, delivered with intent and clarity, it lands. **The formula is simple: one hook + one CTA = clarity.** And in communication, clarity always beats noise.

Mini Exercise — The Flow Test

Take one of your existing carousels — any topic works. Now, restructure it intentionally:

- On slide 1, write a hook that stops the scroll. Something bold, emotional, or curiosity-driven.
- On slide 3 (or the last slide), place a CTA that moves people — "Follow for more," "Save this," or "DM us for details."
- Then preview the flow as if you were the audience.

Does the message guide you smoothly from interest to action? Or does it feel scattered, heavy, or confusing? The goal isn't just to design slides — it's to design behavior. When every visual choice supports a clear psychological path, even the simplest post starts working like a mini sales funnel.

TikTok Posts: Fast, Native, Sticky

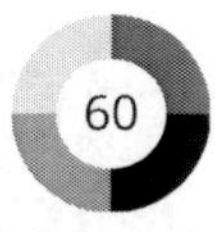

Why this matters.

TikTok thrives on immediacy. Text must live inside safe zones, content must grab attention in 3 seconds, and branding must be subtle but consistent.

Best practices:

- Size: 1080×1920 vertical video.
- Safe zones: avoid bottom third (captions) and right side (engagement buttons).
- Hook: first 3 seconds must stop scroll.
- Logo/branding: small, top corner.

Real Scenario — The Tutor on TikTok

This creator repurposed slides but didn't adjust safe zones—text got covered by captions. After moving text higher, her retention doubled.

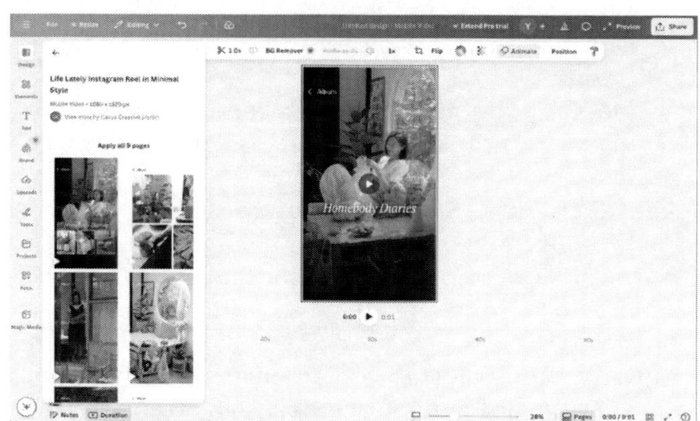

Common Pitfall — Using IG Reels as-is

IG posts often get cut on TikTok. Always adapt composition.

Mini Exercise

Resize one post to 1080×1920. Add bold hook top-center. Export as MP4 and preview.

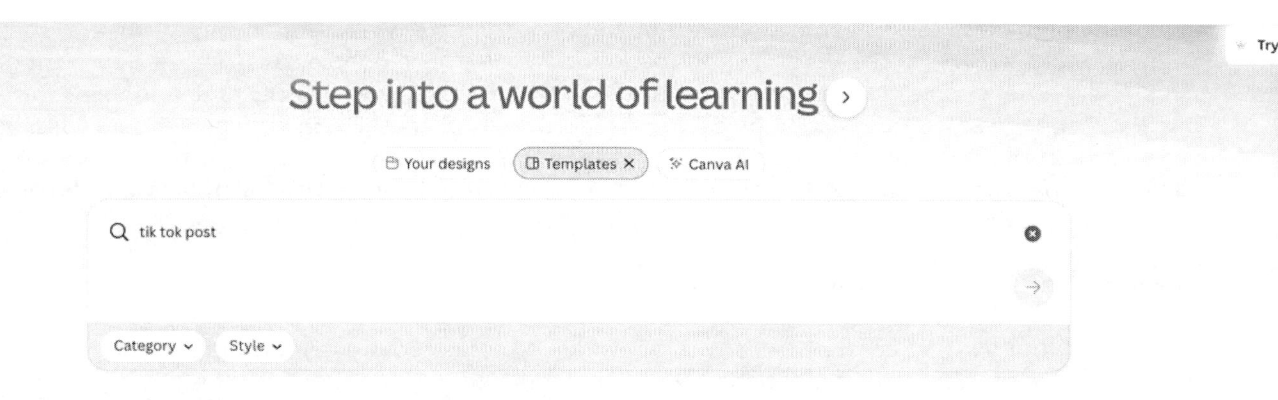

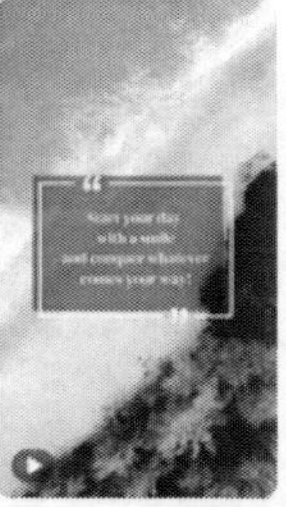
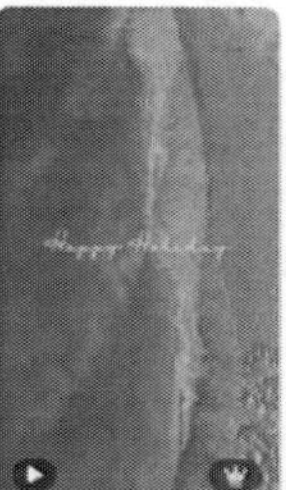

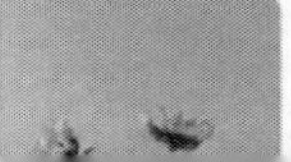

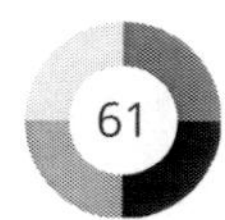

TikTok Stories-Style Sequences: Vertical Flow That Feels Native

Why it matters.

TikTok is built for uninterrupted vertical flow. Whether you have the Stories feature or you're stitching a short multi-clip video, the principle is the same: one idea, broken into clean beats that move quickly and leave no dead air. Your design job isn't to decorate; it's to keep the viewer's attention sliding forward—eyes high, text in safe zones, rhythm alive.

How to build it in Canva (and keep it native).

- Start with 1080×1920. Think in 3–5 beats: Hook → Proof/Visual → Payoff/Tip → CTA.
- Keep each beat to 2–4 seconds.
- Place text above the bottom caption bar and away from the right-side UI (likes/comments/share).
- Use large, high-contrast text and reinforce key words with a subtle highlight box at ~40–60% opacity.
- If you use stickers or polls (when available), leave negative space specifically for them—don't cram them on top of text.

Real Scenario — Micro-Tutorial That Didn't Drag.

A makeup creator turned a 30-second demo into four crisp beats: "Stop cakey under-eye" (hook), close-up of product dab (proof), two-swipe blend with timer overlay (payoff), "Save this for later" (CTA). Watch time jumped, saves spiked, and comments asked for shade recs—because the flow stayed single-task and fast.

Pro Tip — Build a 3-Beat Template.

Create a Canva file with three pages pre-laid: (1) big headline space, (2) mid-screen caption + room for B-roll, (3) oversized CTA with brand color bar. Duplicate for each idea; swap copy and clips. You'll ship twice as fast.

Mini Exercise.

Take one IG Story you already designed. Rebuild it for TikTok as three clips: re-write the headline to 5 words, nudge all text 200–250 px above the bottom edge, and remove any decorative elements near the right edge. Export and preview in TikTok's upload screen to verify nothing is covered.

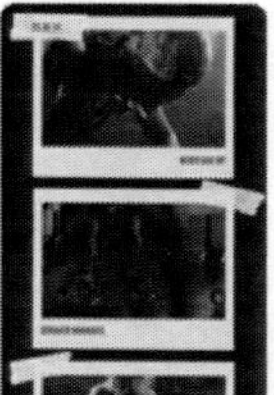

TikTok Carousels (Photo Mode): Swipeable Stories Without Video

Why it matters.

TikTok's Photo Mode (image carousel) lets you tell a story with stills. It's perfect for checklists, step-by-steps, recipes, or before/after sequences when you don't have video. The trap is treating it like a PDF: dense text, tiny type, no pacing. The win is to design it like a comic strip—big beats, one idea per card, and motion implied by the reader's swipe.

How to design it well.

- Create a multi-page 1080×1920 design in Canva: 6–10 cards is a sweet spot.
- Card 1 is a giant hook (promise + outcome)
- Cards 2–n deliver single-bite value (one step, one visual), and the final card is a CTA.
- Use the same type hierarchy across cards so the brain doesn't re-learn your layout each swipe. Keep margins generous, and never drop below 48–56 px for body text in 9:16—remember, thumbs are covering part of the screen.

Real Scenario — "3 Poses for Natural Portraits."

A photographer posted 7 cards: hook, three poses (each with a photo sketch), a "what to avoid" card, gear note, CTA to save. Saves crushed likes 3:1 (a good sign), and comments asked for a lighting sequel. The carousel worked because each card did one job.

Pro Tip — Export as PNGs, Keep Order Tight.

Export cards as individual PNGs labeled 01–10. When uploading to TikTok, keep sequence correct and repeat the hook language in the caption for search.

Mini Exercise.

Turn a 600-word blog tip into 6 cards: Hook → Tip 1 → Tip 2 → Tip 3 → Example → CTA. Design with the same headline size on every card; vary only imagery and subheads. Upload as Photo Mode and test swipe speed yourself.

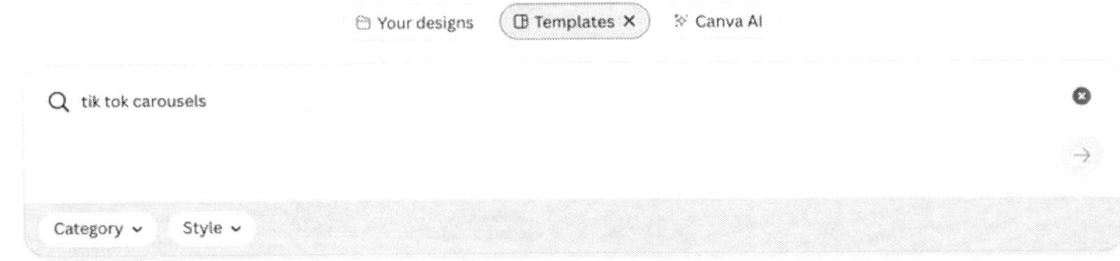

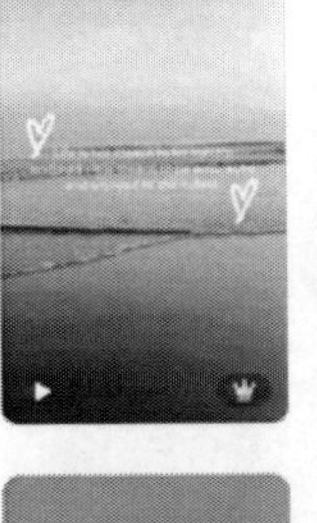

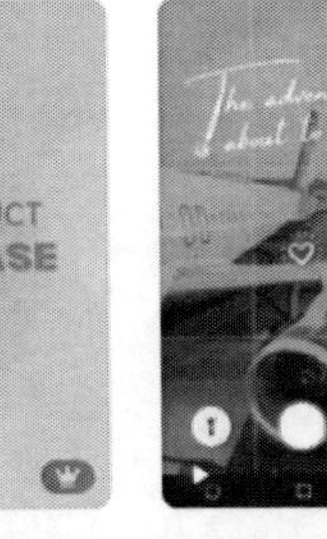
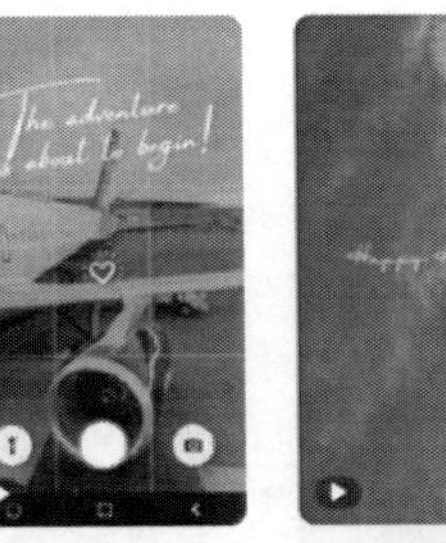
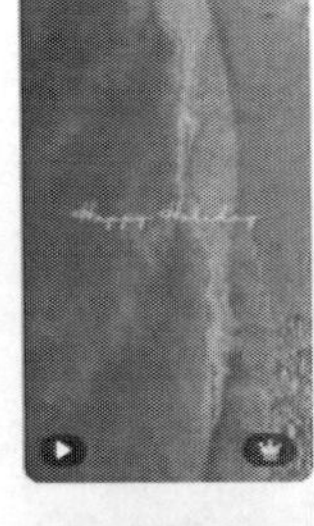

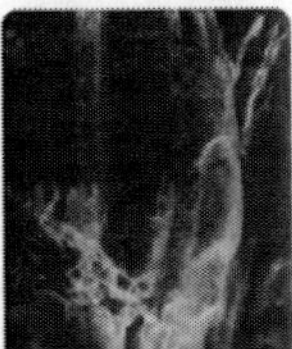

TikTok Covers/Thumbnails: Design the First Frame on Purpose

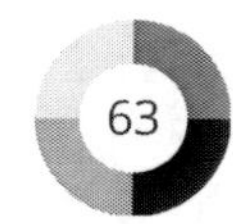

Why it matters.

On TikTok, your "cover" is usually a selected frame with optional text overlay—users meet your video in the grid and on your profile through that tile. If the cover is muddy (tiny type, busy background, words under UI), your best videos underperform. Plan the first frame as a cover, then build the video behind it.

How to do it in Canva (and respect UI).

- Design your opening frame at 1080×1920 with the title in the upper third and centered.
- Leave a clean right edge (TikTok's engagement buttons) and avoid the bottom 250–300 px (caption bar). Keep the title to 3–6 words, high-contrast, and add a small brand mark in the top-left—consistency wins here more than cleverness.

Real Scenario — From Random Frame to Branded Tile.

A fitness coach switched from grabbing a mid-rep frame to a planned first frame: "Fix Your Plank" in big type, clean background, logo top-left. Click-throughs rose because the cover promised a specific outcome you could see at a glance.

Pro Tip — Make a "Cover Grid" Template.

Create one Canva page with faint overlays marking TikTok's right-edge UI and bottom caption area. Use it to compose titles safely. Duplicate for every new video; change only the words and background.

Mini Exercise.

Design three cover variations for the same video: Result-first ("Fix Your Plank"), Problem-first ("Why Your Planks Hurt"), Curiosity ("This Plank Change Feels Wrong—Until It Works"). Export frames and ask a friend which they'd tap. Pick the winner and standardize the style.

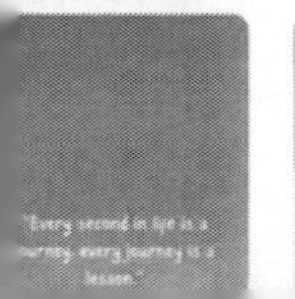

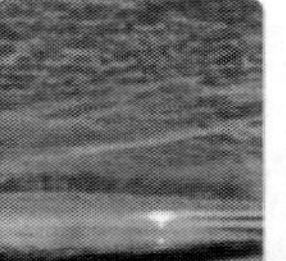

TikTok Hooks & CTAs: Words That Move Thumbs

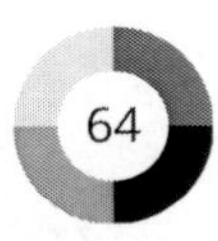

Why it matters.

TikTok's algorithm rewards retention and replays. The hook buys you the first 3 seconds; the CTA converts interest into follows, comments, or saves. Design sets the stage, but language + timing win the watch.

Hooks that work (and why).

- Outcome + Time: "In 10 seconds, fix your color cast." → Clear promise with a clock.
- Stop Doing X: "Stop exporting at 720p." → Pattern interrupt + authority.
- Mistake Reveal: "3 Canva mistakes beginners still make." → Curiosity with built-in value.
- Show, Don't Tell: Start with the after visual, then reveal the before—instant proof.

Place your hook on-screen in the first frame (big type) and say it out loud if you speak on camera—dual-channel hooks stick better. Keep it five to seven words, and make sure the text sits above the caption bar.

CTAs that feel native (not needy).

Use one CTA per video and time it in the final 1–2 seconds: "Save this for your next edit," "Comment 'preset' for the settings," "Follow for the full workflow." Echo the CTA in the caption with a skimmable first line (TikTok surfaces keywords for search).

Real Scenario — Saves Over Likes.

A cooking creator shifted her CTAs from "like and follow" to "save this for Sunday prep." Saves exploded, and so did replays—because the CTA matched user intent.

Pro Tip — Comment Bait That Helps.

Invite a specific response: "Type 'export' if your files look mushy and I'll drop the checklist." You'll drive comments and learn what to make next.

Mini Exercise.

Write five hooks for the same idea, each in 7 words or less. Drop them into your cover frame template and preview on your phone. Pick the one you understand without reading twice—that's your keeper. Then write one CTA that matches the value (save, comment, or follow—not all three).

Checklist — Instagram/TikTok Mastery

- Posts: bold, branded, correct size.
- Stories: one idea per slide, vertical safe zones.
- Carousels: narrative flow, clear hook + CTA.
- TikToks: full-screen, hooks in first 3 seconds, safe zones respected.
- Reels Covers: central safe zone, grid-friendly.
- Hooks & CTAs: sharp, minimal, consistent.

Common Mistakes — And Fixes

- Posts as decoration, not strategy. Fix: always start with hook/CTA in mind.
- Stories overloaded with text. Fix: one idea per slide.
- Carousels too long without rhythm. Fix: alternate text and visuals.
- TikTok ignoring safe zones. Fix: always preview.
- Reel covers messy. Fix: centralize text/logo.

"Do It Now" Homework — 45 Minutes

1. Posts (10 min): Design 3 branded posts with same font/palette.
2. Stories (10 min): Turn one post into 3-slide Story sequence.
3. Carousel (10 min): Build 3 slides with Hook → Value → CTA.
4. TikTok (10 min): Resize one design to 1080×1920, adjust safe zones.
5. Reel Cover (5 min): Create a cover with central safe zone.

QR Bonus (Module Hub):

- Swipe file of 100 Hooks & CTAs tested for social.
- 20 Starter Templates for IG + TikTok.
- Content Pack Calendar (30-day planner).

Closing Thought

Instagram and TikTok aren't just platforms—they're attention machines. If your designs fit natively, respect formats, and lead with strong hooks and CTAs, you don't just look professional—you earn attention, trust, and action. From now on, every post, story, carousel, or reel cover is part of a coherent system: one idea, many formats, one brand.

Chapter 3

YouTube Visuals: Thumbnails, Channel Branding & High-Retention Screens

Chapter 3

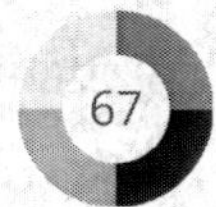

YouTube Visuals: Thumbnails, Channel Branding & High-Retention Screens

On YouTube, your content isn't discovered because it's good—it's discovered because it's clicked. And the click depends almost entirely on the thumbnail. In a crowded sidebar filled with videos, the human brain doesn't read titles first—it scans images. That's why creators say: "The video starts with the thumbnail."

But thumbnails alone don't build trust. When viewers land on your channel, the banner is your storefront. It signals professionalism, niche focus, and whether they should subscribe. And once someone finishes your video, the end screen decides whether they leave or stay in your world. That extra 20 seconds of design can be the difference between one isolated view and a binge session of three or four videos.

Many small creators underestimate this. They spend hours editing content but upload with a random screenshot as a thumbnail, a banner cropped badly on mobile, and no end screen. The result? Low CTR, weak retention, poor growth—even if the content itself is fantastic.

This chapter is about treating YouTube visuals as seriously as the content itself. You'll learn how to:

- Create thumbnails that stop the scroll and raise CTR.
- Design banners that work on desktop, mobile, and TV without cutting text.
- Build end screens that funnel viewers deeper into your channel.
- Adapt content into Shorts with proper safe zones and hooks.

By the end, you won't just have better-looking assets—you'll have a system for YouTube design that earns clicks, builds recognition, and keeps people watching.

What You'll Do in 10 Minutes (and why it matters)

Take a single video idea (e.g., "5 Canva Hacks"):

- Design a thumbnail (1280×720) with a bold headline and one focal image.
- Create a channel banner (2560×1440) with your tagline in the safe area.
- Build a 1920×1080 end screen with placeholders for "Next Video" and "Subscribe."
- Resize one of your IG Stories into a YouTube Short (1080×1920).

Export all four. Place them in one folder called "YouTube Kit." You now have the essential brand system for YouTube—not just a random video upload.

Thumbnails: The Art of the First Impression

Why this matters.

CTR (click-through rate) is one of YouTube's strongest signals. If 10,000 people see your video but only 200 click, the algorithm decides it's not engaging. If 2,000 click, it pushes your video to more people. Thumbnails are the gateway.

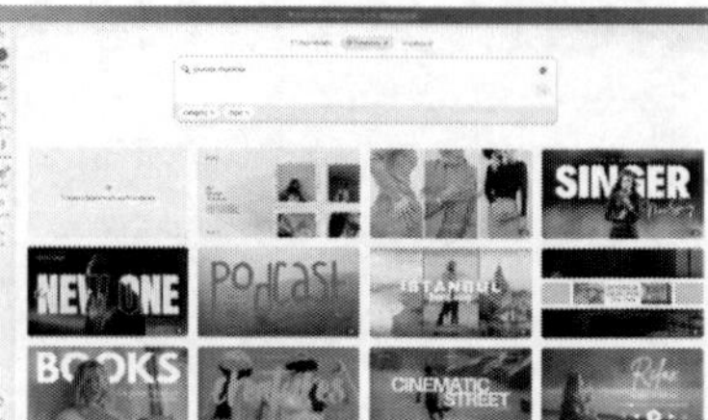

Design Principles:

- Size: 1280×720, always 16:9 ratio.
- Headline: 3–5 words max, large, high-contrast.
- Image: one clear subject (close-up face, product, or bold object).
- Colors: bright or contrasting; use your brand accent consistently.
- Consistency: build a recognisable style so viewers spot your videos instantly.

Real Scenario — Tech Reviewer

A reviewer used bland screenshots for thumbnails. His CTR was under 2%. After redesigning thumbnails with yellow highlights, bold type, and close-up reactions, CTR rose to 6%—triple the clicks, same content.

Pro Tip — The Blink Test

Shrink your thumbnail to 10% size. Can you still read it? If not, simplify text or increase contrast.

Attention — Don't Compete With Titles

Your video title appears right below the thumbnail. Don't repeat it. Use the thumbnail to tease, not to explain.

Common Pitfall — "Poster Syndrome"

Beginners try to cram too much into one thumbnail—multiple images, long sentences, logos everywhere. Result: clutter. The best thumbnails look almost too simple.

Mini Exercise

Design three thumbnail variations for the same video. Change color schemes and headline phrasing. Export and preview at small size. Which one grabs your eye?

Channel Banners: Your Storefront on Every Device

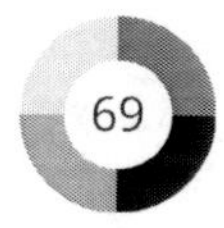

Why this matters.

When viewers click to your channel, they're deciding: "Should I subscribe?" The banner is your brand's handshake. On desktop it's wide, on mobile it's cropped, on TV it's enormous. If you don't respect the safe zone, text gets chopped.

Design Principles:

- Size: 2560×1440.
- Safe Zone: 1546×423 (center strip). Keep all important text here.
- Content: Logo, tagline, upload schedule, maybe social links.
- Tone: Reflect your niche—fun and vibrant for lifestyle, minimal for business, bold for entertainment.

Real Scenario — Fitness Channel

A trainer put "New videos every Monday" at the far right. On mobile, it vanished. After centering it in the safe zone, subs increased—viewers trusted the consistency.

Pro Tip — Schedule Signal

Adding "New videos weekly" or "Tutorials every Tuesday" builds anticipation and loyalty.

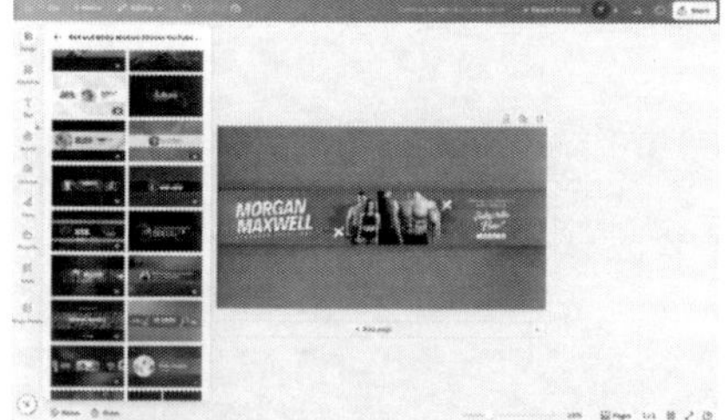

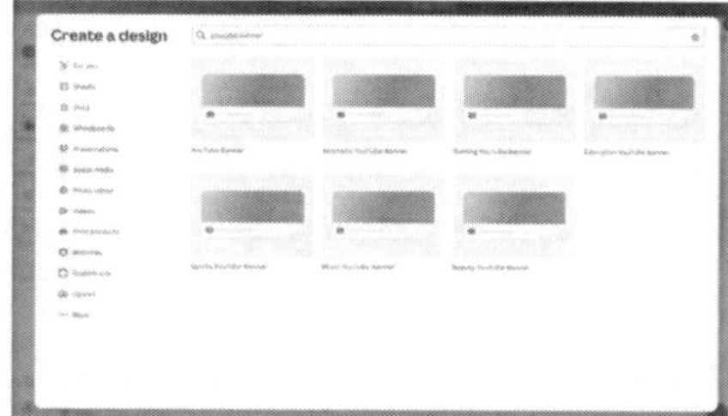

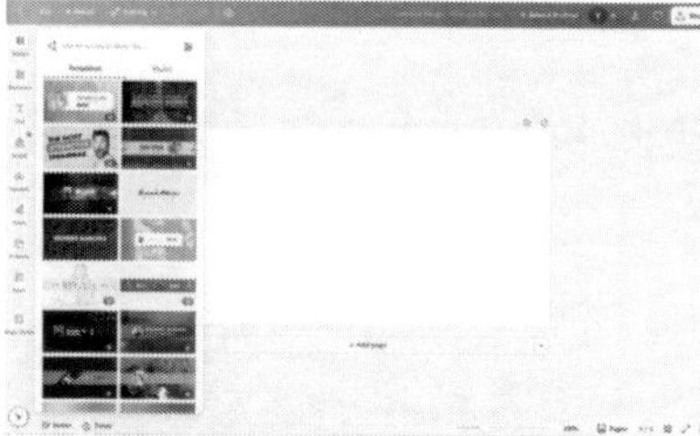

Attention — Mobile First

70% of YouTube traffic is mobile. Always preview your banner in Canva mockups and on your phone.

Common Pitfall — Empty Banners

Some creators leave banners plain or with blurry stock images. It wastes a huge branding opportunity.

Mini Exercise

Design a 2560×1440 banner. Place your logo + tagline in center safe zone. Export and preview on desktop + mobile. Adjust until consistent.

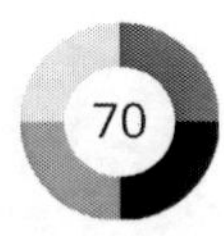

End Screens: Holding Viewers for the Next Step

Why this matters.

Most viewers leave at the end of a video. End screens give them a reason to stay—suggesting another video, playlist, or subscribe button. Retention is key: if viewers watch more of your channel, YouTube rewards you.

Design Principles:

- Size: 1920×1080.
- Placement: Dedicate one side to "Next Video," keep subscribe button in same spot across all videos.
- Background: gradient, brand color, or blurred video still.
- Text: simple CTA ("Watch Next," "Subscribe for More").

Real Scenario — Gaming Creator

A social media manager ended videos with black screen. Viewers dropped instantly. After adding bright end screens with fun CTAs, watch time rose 15%.

Pro Tip — Branded Template

Make one end screen layout in Canva. Reuse it for all videos. Consistency = recognition.

Attention — Too Many Options

Offering four links overwhelms viewers. Keep it to one "Next Video" and one "Subscribe."

Mini Exercise

Design a 1920×1080 end screen. Add a "Watch Next" area and "Subscribe" icon. Export and overlay on a test clip.

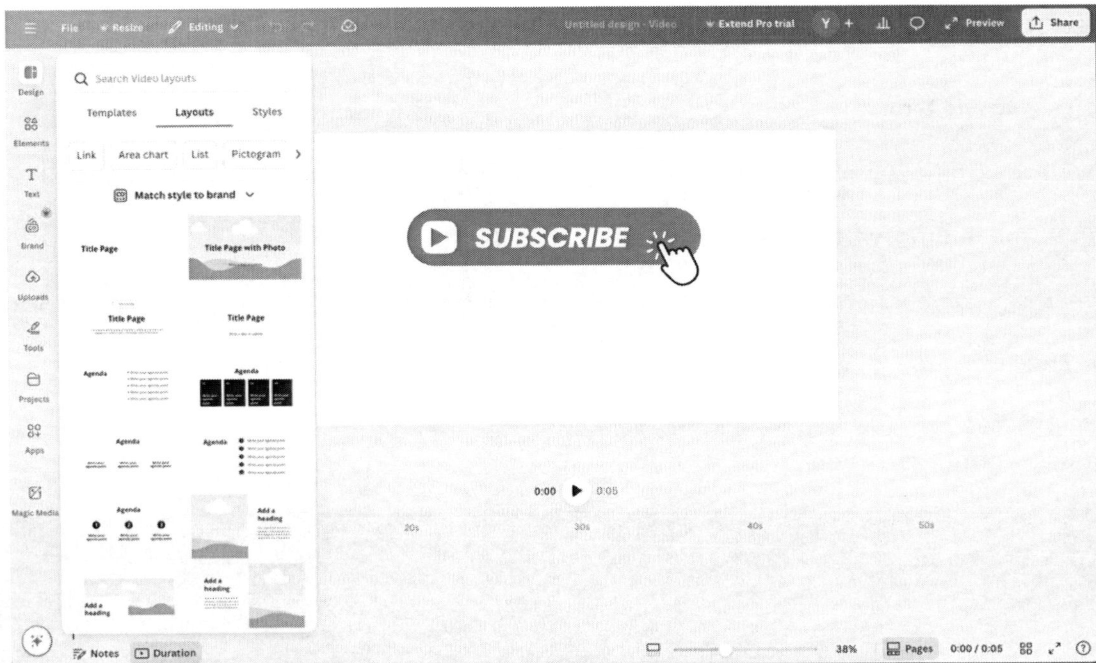

Shorts: YouTube's Answer to TikTok

Why this matters.

YouTube Shorts (1080×1920) drive massive exposure. They appear in a separate feed and reach audiences who may never see your long videos. Shorts thrive on hooks in the first 3 seconds.

Design Principles:

- Size: 1080×1920 vertical.
- Safe zones: avoid bottom caption + top cropping.
- Hooks: place big text top-center.
- CTA: add "Subscribe for full video" at end.

Real Scenario — Educator

A creator clipped 30-second moments from lectures, added bold titles, and posted as Shorts. Subscriber growth tripled.

Pro Tip — Reuse Stories

IG Story templates adapt perfectly into Shorts. Just adjust for YouTube's pacing.

Mini Exercise

Take one IG Story. Resize into 1080×1920 Short. Add bold headline at top. Export and preview.

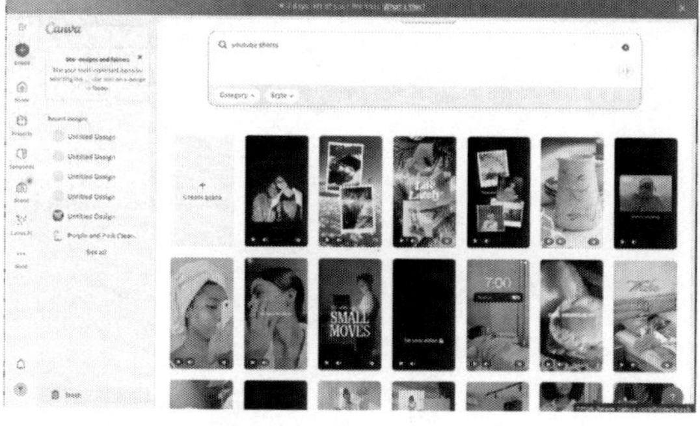

Closing Thought

A strong thumbnail earns the click. A clean banner builds trust. An end screen extends retention. Shorts expand reach. Together, they form a design system that amplifies your content.

Checklist — YouTube Design Kit

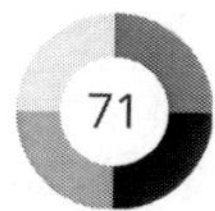

- Thumbnails: bold, short text, clear focal point, brand accent.
- Banner: safe zone respected, tagline centered.
- End screens: consistent template, max two CTAs.
- Shorts: hooks in first 3 seconds, safe zone text.

Common Mistakes — And How to Fix Them

- Thumbnail text too long. Fix: keep ≤5 words.
- Banner text cut on mobile. Fix: stay inside safe zone.
- End screens overcrowded. Fix: stick to two CTAs.
- Shorts without hooks. Fix: add bold opening headline.

"Do It Now" Homework — 60 Minutes

1. Thumbnail Sprint (20 min): Create 3 thumbnail variations for one video. Test at small size.
2. Banner Build (15 min): Design banner with tagline and upload schedule. Test on phone.
3. End Screen Layout (15 min): Create branded template. Save for reuse.
4. Shorts Adaptation (10 min): Repurpose one Story as a Short.

QR Bonus (Module Hub):

- 5 Thumbnail Templates (CTR-tested).
- Banner Safe Zone Guide.
- Reusable End Screen Template.
- Shorts Storyboard Template.

Chapter 4

Planning & Batching: Reusable Systems, Weekly Calendars & Smart Libraries

Chapter 4

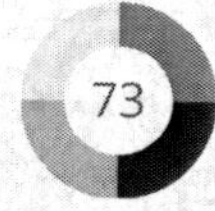

Planning & Batching: Reusable Systems, Weekly Calendars & Smart Libraries

Scroll through the feeds of the creators or businesses you admire most. You'll notice something: their content feels planned. Posts appear in rhythm, stories connect to promotions, carousels drop on the same day each week, and there's no sense of panic. It feels like they're always prepared.

Now contrast that with the average beginner's feed: bursts of activity followed by silence, a random motivational quote next to a blurry product shot, stories that feel improvised. The difference isn't creativity—it's systems. Professionals don't sit down each day asking "What should I post?" They already know, because they've batched, scheduled, and built libraries that do half the work for them.

This chapter is about building your hidden engine. Canva gives you the tools—duplication, content planner, and folders—but the mindset is what matters: stop reinventing, start scaling. With duplication, you multiply designs quickly. With a planner, you turn designs into a timeline. With libraries, you create a system that accelerates every future session.

By the end, you'll have a repeatable workflow:

- One idea becomes five posts in minutes.
- A month of content sits ready, mapped and labeled.
- Your future self doesn't hunt for logos, colors, or CTAs—they're already in place.

This is how creators free up time, small businesses look professional, and social media managers stay sane. Consistency isn't luck. It's a machine. And you're about to build it.

What You'll Do in 10 Minutes (and why it matters)

- Pick one post design.
- Duplicate it 5 times.
- On each version, change just one thing—headline, image, background color, CTA box, layout spacing. Export the set.

You've just created a micro-pack of content. What seemed like "one post" has become "a week of posts." That small shift in thinking—system, not scramble—is the foundation of every social brand that grows.

Duplication: More Posts, Less Effort

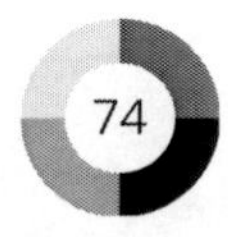

Why this matters.

Beginners often confuse "original" with "effective." In reality, audiences don't need a brand-new layout every day. They need clarity and repetition. Duplication saves time, keeps style consistent, and allows you to focus on message instead of decoration.

How to do it.

- Start with a master design. Build one strong post that feels aligned with your brand.
- Duplicate inside Canva. Click "Duplicate page" or "Make a copy."
- Vary one element per version. Example: headline text, background color, image, or CTA phrasing.
- Batch export. Export all in one folder, naming clearly (Post01, Post02...).

Real Scenario — The Online Coach

An online coach used to design every single post from scratch. It took hours. Once she started duplicating and varying one element, she produced 15 posts in the same time it used to take her to make 3. Her audience didn't see "repetition"—they saw a consistent brand voice.

Pro Tip — Theme Packs

Instead of single posts, think in packs: "5 Tips," "3 Myths," "4 Quotes." Duplicating the design gives you a family of content that feels coherent.

Attention — Cosmetic vs Strategic Variation

Don't change so much that the posts feel random. Small, consistent shifts build rhythm. Keep fonts, logos, and layout steady.

Mini Exercise — The 5-Variation Sprint

Take one design. Duplicate it five times. Version A: new headline. Version B: new image. Version C: rotate brand color. Version D: change CTA box. Version E: adjust spacing. Export all and compare side by side. Do they look like siblings?

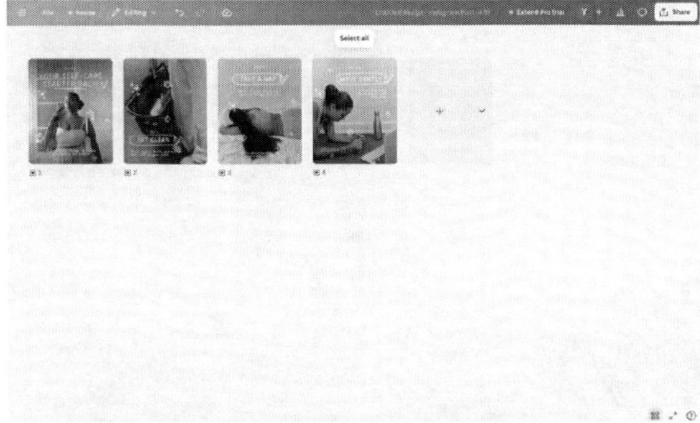

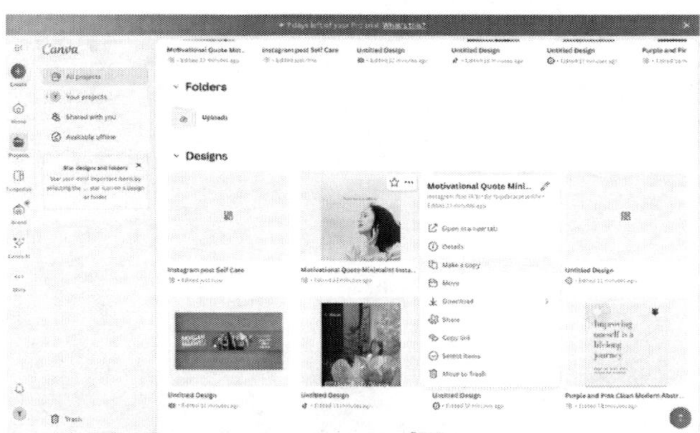

Calendars: Turning Designs Into Strategy

Why this matters.

Great content dies if it's not posted at the right time. A content calendar shifts you from "reactive" to "proactive." Instead of waking up to design something for today, you map your month in advance. This creates rhythm, variety, and space for creativity where it matters.

How to use Canva's Content Planner.

Inside Canva, after finishing a design, click "Share → Schedule." Pick your platform, write your caption, and set the date. Repeat for your batch of posts. In the Planner view, you'll see a monthly grid filled with your scheduled designs.

How to do it manually.

If you prefer external tools, export your posts, drop them in a folder labeled by month (e.g., "Nov 2025 Social Pack"), and create a Google Sheet with columns: Date, Platform, Theme, Post File. This gives you control across multiple platforms.

Real Scenario — Local Bakery

The bakery used to post whenever they remembered. Engagement was low. After mapping a calendar—Mondays for product highlights, Wednesdays for tips, Fridays for promotions—their audience started expecting content. Customers even messaged on Fridays waiting for the new promo post.

Pro Tip — Theme Days for Momentum

Assigning categories to days prevents burnout: "Motivation Monday," "Tip Tuesday," "Feature Friday." Audiences love rhythm, and you design faster when categories are fixed.

Common Pitfall — Overstuffed Calendars

Ambition kills consistency. Don't plan 50 posts if you can realistically create 20. Consistency beats volume.

Mini Exercise — Build a Month View

Take 12 designs. Assign them to a monthly grid (either in Canva Planner or Google Sheets). Label by theme. Export the calendar and pin it above your desk.

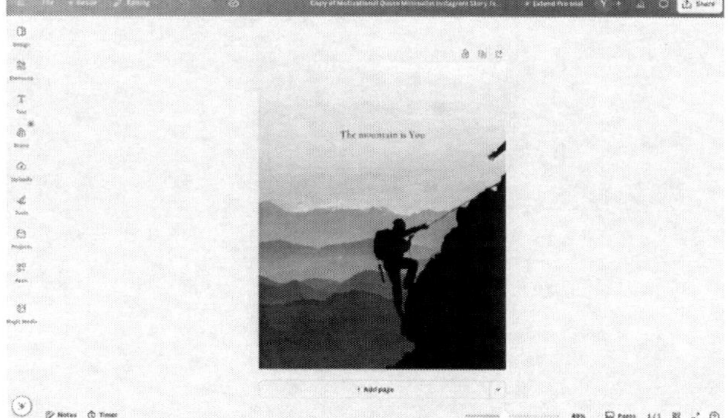

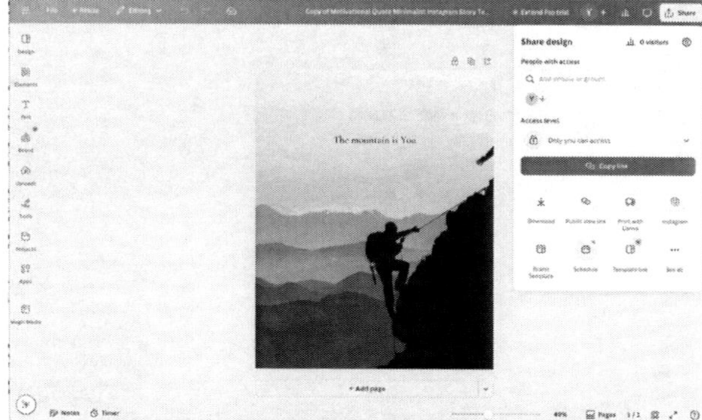

Libraries: Your Personal Design Warehouse

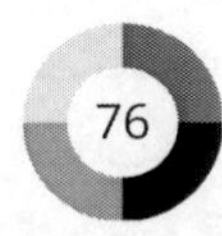

Why this matters.

Imagine cooking a meal where every time you had to find a new knife, pan, or ingredient from scratch. That's how beginners treat Canva: every session, they search for logos, fonts, colors, icons. A library turns chaos into flow.

How to do it.

- **Brand Kit**: If you have Canva Pro, load your fonts, colors, and logos once. Every new design starts branded.
- **Folders**: Create folders for Photos, Icons, Overlays, Carousels, Reels. Label them clearly.
- **Components page**: Build one Canva page with reusable assets—CTA buttons, dividers, overlays. Copy them into new projects.

Real Scenario — Content Creator

A content creator wasted 20 minutes each session hunting for the "right" arrow icon. After making a components page with her go-to icons and overlays, design time dropped by 50%.

Pro Tip — Star What You Actually Use

In Canva, you can "Star" assets. Do this for icons, photos, and templates you love. Your starred items become a quick library inside search.

Attention — Clean the Clutter

A messy library slows you down. Once a month, archive unused elements. The less you see, the faster you choose.

Mini Exercise — Build Your Library Now

Create a folder called "Brand Library." Add your logo, brand colors, and 10 reusable icons. Create one "Components Page" with at least 3 overlays and 2 CTA buttons. Star them all.

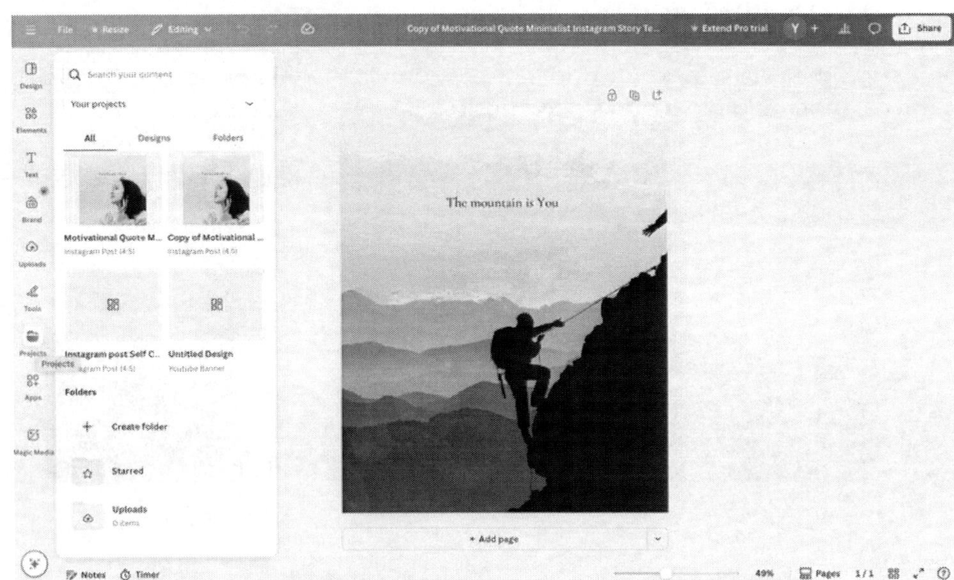

Connecting the Three: Duplication + Calendar + Library

Why this matters.

Each element is powerful on its own, but the system comes alive when they work together:

- Duplication produces volume.
- The calendar organizes that volume.
- The library speeds up creation each time.

Together, they form a loop: design once, multiply, schedule, repeat faster.

Real Scenario — Marketing Agency Workflow

A small agency created 40 posts for a client in two days by combining these three: duplicated templates, scheduled them in Canva Planner, and pulled assets from a pre-built brand library. What looked like magic was simply systems.

Mini Exercise — The Loop Test

Pick one design. Duplicate 5 versions. Assign them to dates. Export to your Brand Library folder. You've just run the cycle once. Repeat monthly, and posting becomes routine instead of stress.

Checklist — Planner & Batch Mastery

1. One design can be multiplied into 5–10 variants.
2. Posts are mapped into a monthly calendar.
3. Themes assigned to days (tips, promos, quotes, stories).
4. Library built with logos, fonts, palette, reusable icons and overlays.
5. Components page ready for fast duplication.
6. Workflow loop established: Duplicate → Schedule → Store.

Common Mistakes — And How to Fix Them

- Designing from scratch every time. → Fix: Duplicate and vary.
- Random posting. → Fix: Use planner or spreadsheet.
- Cluttered library. → Fix: Clean monthly, star essentials.
- Overambitious calendars. → Fix: Plan realistically, then scale.
- Inconsistent logos/colors. → Fix: Always use Brand Kit or Brand Library.

"Do It Now" Homework — 60 Minutes

1. 5-Variation Pack (15 min).
2. Choose one design. Duplicate 5 versions with slight changes. Export as "Variation Pack."
3. Monthly Calendar (20 min).
4. Take 12 designs. Assign them to specific dates (via Canva Planner or Google Sheets). Add categories (Tip, Testimonial, Promo).
5. Brand Library Setup (15 min).
6. Create folder with logo, fonts, swatches, 10 icons. Add a Components page with CTA buttons + overlays.
7. Run the Loop (10 min).
8. Take one variation, schedule it in Canva Planner, store it in your folder. Repeat for 3 posts.
9. QR Bonus (Module Hub):
10. 30-Day Content Calendar Template (Google Sheet + Canva).
11. 20 Batch-Ready Templates.
12. Reusable Components Kit.
13. Brand Library Folder Starter Pack.

Closing Thought

Calendars save your consistency. Libraries save your energy. Build this once, and your creative work stops being a daily struggle and starts being a machine that runs smoothly.

Chapter 5

Publishing Basics: Naming, CTR Awareness & Version Control

Chapter 5

Publishing Basics: Naming, CTR Awareness & Version Control

In this chapter, we go from pretty pictures to measurable results. There's a hard truth in the world of digital content: nobody cares how much time you spent designing a post. The only thing that matters is whether the post worked. **But how do you define "worked"? Was it about likes? Comments? Shares?** For a designer, those numbers may feel validating. Yet for a brand or a business, the real indicator is whether the design moved someone to act. Did they click? Did they open? Did they watch? Did they move one step deeper into your ecosystem?

This is where metrics come in—not as cold numbers, but as the mirror that reflects how your audience reacts to your work. Metrics transform design from an artistic exercise into a growth engine. They don't kill creativity; they guide it. They help you distinguish between what looks good to you and what actually works for your audience.

The most important of these is CTR—Click-Through Rate. CTR is the lifeline of design on digital platforms. A carousel that gets people swiping, a thumbnail that makes someone click play, a story that drives a tap forward—CTR is the thread connecting your visual to the next action. You could think of it as the heartbeat of your design: if it's strong, the design is alive; if it's weak, the design is flat.

But numbers without order are noise. That's why naming conventions and versioning strategies matter just as much. If you don't name your files properly, you'll never know which design produced which result. If you don't version systematically, you'll never learn what change improved performance. Without these practices, your "data" is useless—just a cloud of posts you can't trace.

And then comes publishing. Publishing is not just pressing "post." It's about rhythm. It's about telling a story in time, building anticipation, creating predictability for your audience and reliability for algorithms. A publishing schedule is a silent signal: "We're serious, we're here, and you can trust us to show up."
In this chapter, you'll discover how metrics, naming, versioning, and publishing work together to turn chaos into clarity.

We'll explore how to track CTR and use it as design feedback, how to build a naming system that makes analytics usable, how to version like a scientist, and how to publish with rhythm instead of randomness.

By the end, you won't just design posts—you'll design outcomes.

CTR: The Metric That Speaks the Loudest

Why this matters.

Imagine two posts: one garners 1,000 likes but only 3 link clicks. The other has 200 likes but 50 clicks. Which one did its job? The second. CTR cuts through the vanity of "vanity metrics." It's not about applause—it's about action.

The anatomy of CTR.

On Instagram, CTR might show up as "Profile Visits" or "Website Clicks." On YouTube, it's thumbnail CTR—impressions vs actual views. On LinkedIn, it's clicks on a carousel PDF. CTR is always the ratio between exposure and action: how many saw it, and how many cared enough to act.

Real Scenario — The Webinar Flyer

A coach designed a beautiful post crammed with details: date, time, benefits, testimonials. CTR was 0.7%. When she stripped it down to a bold headline, one key benefit, and a clean CTA button, CTR shot up to 3.5%. The offer didn't change—only the design did.

Pro Tip — Treat CTR as Creative Feedback

Low CTR isn't an insult. It's feedback. Maybe the headline was too small, maybe the CTA button blended in, maybe the image was irrelevant. Each low CTR is a clue.

Common Pitfall — Blaming the Algorithm

It's easy to say, "The platform doesn't like me." But often, the audience didn't see value quickly enough. CTR forces you to confront that gap.

Mini Exercise — A/B Testing for Designers

Take one post. Create two versions: Version A with headline focus, Version B with image focus. Publish both. After a week, compare CTR. Write down two lessons from the results—what worked, what didn't. This turns every post into a learning lab.

Naming: Order in the Midst of Chaos

Why this matters.

Without naming conventions, you're lost in the wilderness. Files called "final-final-v3.jpg" don't tell you anything. Six months later, you won't remember what that file was, let alone how it performed. Naming conventions create traceability. They allow you to connect designs to metrics and learn over time.

How to name with purpose.

Adopt a formula: Date + Platform + Campaign + Version.

- Example: 2025-10_IG_FocusTips_V1.jpg
- Carousel example: 2025-10_LI_CarouselProduct_V2_Slide03.pdf

Real Scenario — The Agency in Chaos

A small agency couldn't tell which designs had worked for a client. CTR reports came in, but they didn't know which visuals they referred to. After enforcing naming rules, they matched performance to specific designs and doubled down on what worked.

Attention — Naming as Future-Proofing

Don't name for today. Name for six months from now, when you've forgotten. Name for the colleague who will join your team. Name for the campaign you'll revisit next year.

Mini Exercise — Build a Named Set

Create 3 posts. Save them with naming convention: 2025-10_IG_Mindset_V1, 2025-10_IG_Mindset_V2, 2025-10_IG_Mindset_V3. Drop them in a folder. Notice how clarity emerges instantly.

Versioning: The Designer's Science Lab

Why this matters.

Great design isn't guessing—it's iteration. Versioning means creating small, deliberate variations to test what works. It's design turned into science.

The rules of versioning.

- Change one variable at a time: color, image, headline.
- Label clearly: V1, V2, V3.
- Publish or schedule side by side.
- Record results.

Real Scenario — The SaaS Startup

A startup tested two thumbnails: one with founder's smiling face, one with abstract illustration. CTR on face: 8%. CTR on illustration: 3%. From then on, they always used faces.

Pro Tip — Document Every Test

Use a simple spreadsheet: Date, Platform, Campaign, Version, CTR, Notes. Over time, patterns emerge—like "faces beat objects" or "yellow outperforms blue."

Common Pitfall — Changing Too Much

If you change font, color, image, and text all at once, you won't know which caused the result. Discipline in versioning is everything.

Mini Exercise — Three Versions, Three Lessons

Create three versions of the same post: V1 with color change, V2 with font change, V3 with image change. Export, name properly, and track.

Publishing: Rhythm Builds Trust

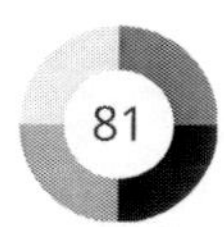

Why this matters.

Random posting feels chaotic to audiences and invisible to algorithms. Consistency, not volume, is what builds trust. A publishing rhythm makes you predictable—in a good way.

The publishing mindset.

Think of publishing as music. The posts are notes, but the schedule is the rhythm. Without rhythm, it's noise. With rhythm, it's a song your audience learns to expect.

How to execute.

- Use Canva's Content Planner to assign dates.
- Or export posts into folders and schedule with tools like Buffer, Later, or Meta Business Suite.
- Better to post 3× a week consistently than 7× in one week and silence the next.

Real Scenario — The Lifestyle Blogger

A creator posted sporadically: three posts in one week, then nothing for a month. Engagement lagged. After scheduling weekly posts in Canva, her audience began to anticipate her content. "Love your Monday tips!" followers said. Predictability became part of her brand.

Pro Tip — Build Cadence, Not Perfection

Don't obsess over "best times." Algorithms reward consistent presence. Your brand's heartbeat matters more than timing tricks.

Mini Exercise — Map a Week

Take 5 designs. Schedule them across one week in Canva Planner. Preview the calendar. Notice the relief that comes with clarity.

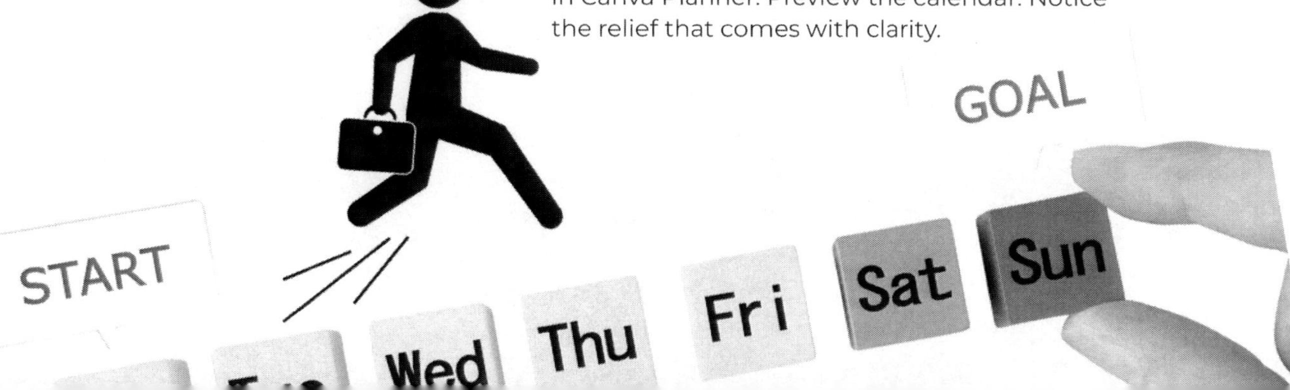

Checklist: From Chaos to System

- CTR is tracked regularly, not ignored.
- Naming conventions applied to all files.
- Versioning done with discipline (one variable per change).
- Publishing rhythm established (weekly cadence).
- Planner or spreadsheet used to schedule.

Common Mistakes — And How to Fix Them

- Focusing on likes instead of CTR. Solution: train yourself to look at actions, not applause.
- Files with random names. Solution: enforce naming conventions.
- Testing too many variables. Solution: one change at a time.
- Posting when inspired only. Solution: set rhythm, not mood.

"Do It Now" Homework — 60 Minutes

1. CTR Test (20 min).
2. Design two versions of the same post. Publish both. After one week, compare CTR and write down 3 lessons.
3. Naming Audit (10 min).
4. Take 10 of your existing files. Rename them using the convention: Date + Platform + Campaign + Version.
5. Versioning Sprint (15 min).
6. Create three versions of one design: change only one element each. Save with V1, V2, V3.
7. Publishing Rhythm (15 min).
8. Map out a week of content. Assign each post to a day in Canva Planner or a Google Sheet.

QR Bonus (Module Hub):

- CTR Tracking Sheet (Google Doc).
- Naming & Versioning Guide.
- Weekly Publishing Calendar Template.

Closing Thought

Design is only half the job. The other half is learning from results, organizing your work, and showing up with rhythm. Metrics are your compass, naming is your map, versioning is your experiment, and publishing is your drumbeat. Master these, and your social media stops being guesswork—it becomes growth.

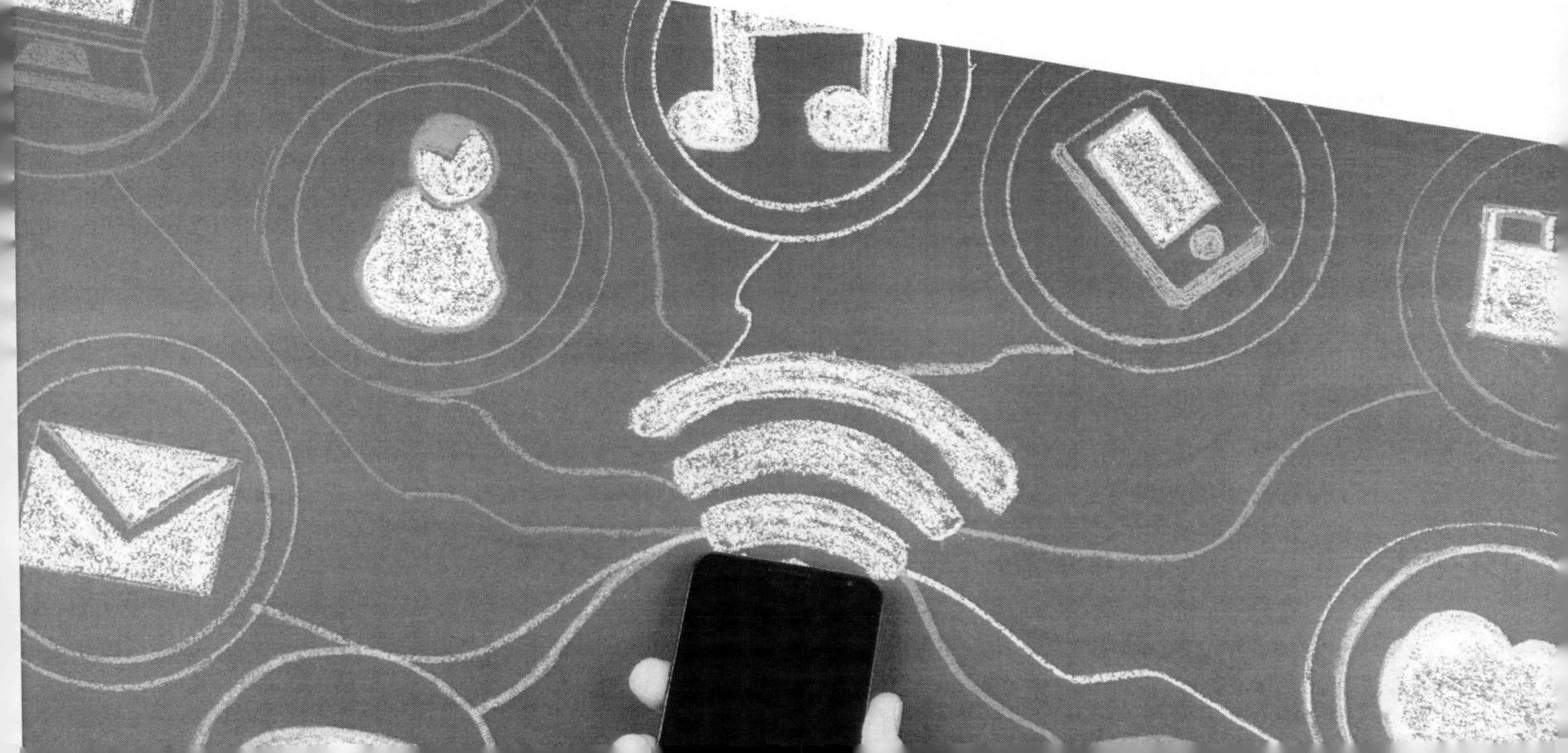

Conclusion:

From Your First Post to Your First Creative Voice

When you opened this book, Canva might have felt like unfamiliar territory, a place full of buttons, tools, and templates where it was easy to get lost. But page after page, **you've seen something different**: design isn't about being perfect, it's about being clear, intentional, and consistent. And consistency, especially on social media, is what turns beginners into recognizable creators.

You didn't need complicated software or years of experience to get here. You needed a starting point: and now you have one. You've learned how to set up your Canva space, choose colors and fonts that make sense, design layouts that feel clean, work with images that support your message, and export posts that look sharp on every platform.

These are not small steps. They're the **foundations** that make every future post easier, faster, and more natural.

The real shift, though, is not technical, it's creative. You now understand how to build visuals that carry your voice. You know how to guide the viewer's eye, how to make a carousel flow, how to create a post that stops the scroll. And you know how to repeat that process tomorrow, next week, next month, without starting from zero each time.

If you keep practicing what you've learned, **Canva won't feel like a tool anymore.** It will feel like a place where your ideas take shape. And remember: every creator you admire online started exactly where you are now. With a first post. With a first attempt. With a design that wasn't perfect. What matters is showing up with intention and allowing your style to grow.

- So open Canva again.
- Create something small.
- Try a new color, a new layout, a new hook.

Every post teaches you something, and every step brings you closer to the creative voice you're building.

Also, along the way, you've seen QR codes woven through the chapters — small shortcuts that turned each lesson into something you could apply immediately.

You're ready for it. You can design this. And you're just getting started.

Turning Skills Into Creative Practice

Your Social Media Starter Toolkit

You've reached the end of this book — and that already tells me a lot. Beginners don't always finish guides; creators do. And now that you've learned the fundamentals, it's time to put them into practice.

Inside your toolkit you'll find simple, ready-to-use resources designed to help you move from learning to creating. They're not advanced tools — they're friendly shortcuts you can duplicate and adapt to your own style as you grow.

You'll find:

- Templates you can customize for posts and carousels
- Checklists to keep your designs clean and consistent
- Mini-guides that help you plan ideas and schedule your content
- Quick prompts to inspire captions, hooks, and social frames
- And yes — there's even a full **BONUS CONTENT on Canva for Video Editing** to help you take your visuals into motion. **--->**

You'll recognize these resources by the QR codes included in this book. Scan them, open them in Canva, and modify them freely. The more you use them, the faster the design process will feel.

The real value isn't in collecting templates — it's in applying them. Try them out. Adjust them. Make them fit your voice. The goal isn't perfection; it's progress. After each chapter, revisit the bonus material and turn what you learned into a real post. By the time you finish experimenting with everything inside this toolkit, you won't just understand how Canva works — **you'll have built the beginnings of a personal creative system you can grow over time.**

This is your moment to take the first step from "beginner" to "creator." Now, bring your ideas to life.

Made in United States
North Haven, CT
04 February 2026